Aude Lo

Juliette

A mother's story of hope in the face of adversity

Printed in the United Kingdom
Revised Edition

ISBN: 978-1-3999-1735-3

Published independently

Email: author@juliettebook.com

Website: www.juliettebook.com

Cover illustration: Begoña Anson Lorente
email: bansonlorente@gmail.com

Editorial Production: The Editor's Chair

*In memory of Juliette, Cassie, Kyle,
Robert Donald, Maisie and Reuben.*

*And to all our children who we miss here on earth,
carrying the hope we will meet again in heaven.*

Contents

Introduction

Why I wrote this book

"Aude and Baptiste lost a child who had trisomy 13."
This is how most people would summarise our story. Our
reality is far vaster and richer. To shorten our story to these
ten words would mean missing out on our journey. Who
was Juliette, our child? What did we learn through her?
This book shares our story by our precious daughter's
side, a journey made as a family, profound and painful,
but also full of joy and revelation.

This book reflects my own experiences as a mother,
infused with all that Baptiste, my husband, and I faced
hand-in-hand. We went through this experience together,
in a different and yet complementary way. Through these
writings, I wanted to tell you of how I experienced these
things personally.

I would also like this book to be an encouragement
for parents going through similar situations, an
encouragement for them to meet their child even when
the medical prognosis suggests that he or she will not
survive after birth. This is precisely what we were faced
with and yet we were able to experience something
unique and remarkable with our daughter. Even if Juliette
died eight months into the pregnancy, we can say today
that we really met her. We know our daughter, we have
perceived her character, her destiny; and that really makes

a difference. Life is precious. There is something to grasp and understand in each event. Thanks to Juliette, a path has opened up in our hearts, and our lives have been profoundly transformed.

Inspiration

Not long after the birth of our first child Raphaël, I was very taken with the story of Alyssa and Chris. This couple, both leaders of a church in California, lost a child in their 40th week of pregnancy. I remember following their story, carrying my child in my arms, who was only a few months old, and being drawn in, feeling almost connected to their situation without knowing them and without my current reality resembling theirs. I felt connected to their pain, to the grieving process they were preparing to go on, without knowing that we too would face the same sort of situation a year later.

When I knew about Juliette's condition, the memory of their story came back to me. I especially remembered that Alyssa mentioned a book she was writing. This book, which I read during my pregnancy, was like an anchor for my soul. Knowing that a couple, firmly rooted in faith, had also gone down this road without being destroyed, gave me the strength and perseverance to look for the best throughout the ordeal we were going through ourselves.

I hope that my book will have the same reach, that it will help others who are facing a similar situation.

Meet our family

Baptiste and I met in Paris. From the beginning, I was struck by his maturity and wisdom. He always has the right words, the words that bring comfort and reassurance. I have a lot of admiration and respect for his sensitivity and thoughtfulness. We were friends for three years before falling in love with each other. As soon as I had feelings for him, I instantly knew he was the love of my life. Since then, that confidence has been unwavering. Our story as a couple began under the Tuscan sun in Italy. It is there that we also shared our vision for the family we wanted to build, a welcoming one, full of life and a source of joy for us and those around us. We wanted it to be open so that people would feel like they were at home, that they would feel welcome and loved. This description could seem mundane and actually quite commonplace, but it echoed in both of us. It was this dimension of joy beyond the day-to-day that we were drawn to. A joy, which can be expressed beyond difficult circumstances. This joy underlies our family life even if it isn't always visible. Being able to just rejoice, having a thankful heart, without being influenced by circumstances or by emotions, was our common goal. Life certainly hasn't spared me from difficult situations, but I have always looked to discern the best, the positive in what can sometimes seem dark and void of hope.

We got married in the summer of 2012, outside in nature, amongst the vines and valleys of Beaujolais. We celebrated our union for three days, surrounded by our loved ones. It was an authentic, simple, and glorious time.

In June 2015, we became parents to our first child, Raphaël. Words cannot describe the fullness that I felt. I had an ideal pregnancy, so happy to know that a little person was being created day after day inside of me. We practiced *haptonomie*, a method that encourages a link with the child through contact, from four months of pregnancy.[1] Raphaël, our adorable blonde with blue eyes, never ceases to amaze and impress us with his numerous

---

1   V. Frans Veldman, *Haptonomie*, science de l'affectivité, P.U.F., 2007.

exploits. He is very attentive and observes everything around him. He loves music and, at two years old, he can already recognise instruments when he hears a piece of music. He's also fascinated with everything on wheels. He is very fast; the balance bike and scooter hold no secrets for him! With him, we became parents. With him, our house was filled with laughter, song, and dance.

In September 2016, we were filled with joy again as we found out that I was pregnant with our second child. The symptoms of pregnancy hit almost immediately, and the test only confirmed what I already felt. Not long after this wonderful news, we moved to Scotland. As we love travelling, discovering a new country, and simultaneously welcoming this new life being knit inside of me seemed like pure joy.

As with Raphaël, being pregnant, knowing this child was growing, was a source of immense gratitude and peace. Raphaël's pregnancy went wonderfully and for me, it seemed obvious that it would be the same for every one of my children.

Pregnant with Juliette

News of the diagnosis

We waited impatiently for the 20-week scan, to see pictures of our child and also to find out if we were having a girl or a boy. I didn't think for one second that the ultrasound would highlight a problem. So, I was not at all prepared for what was to come. This scan surely would not highlight anything unusual; the baby's heart would be beating well, and the measurements would be perfect. Our assurance was even stronger given that my first pregnancy went smoothly without the tiniest complication. Pregnancy is good news, we are welcoming a new life so why worry? For a parent, the worst is always unimaginable.

Yet, getting into the car going to the maternity unit, a tiny grain of sand slips into my thoughts in a split second. I have the impression that something 'isn't right', without really knowing what and without giving it much notice. It is like the wind changing direction without warning. I tell myself that this slight feeling is because I am in a new country, with a different health care system: that's probably what is bringing up this feeling of uncertainty.

So, here we are at our ultrasound appointment, impatient to see our child, to hear the heartbeat, and to marvel at every detail of this young life captured on screen.

At the start, the ultrasound seems to go normally. The scan shows that we are expecting a girl. We rejoice at this news, and we start to imagine Raphaël as a big brother to a little sister. However, as the practitioner takes more measurements, she seems to notice something unusual. We find out that the measurements are causing an issue, without anyone being able to tell us why. The specialist goes to consult her team and she explains that one concern is the baby is small for 20 weeks. That doesn't seem that alarming to us, given that she still has lots of time left to grow! We're not that worried either because we've just moved to Scotland, and we know that they count the weeks a little differently to France. So, we tell ourselves it must just be down to a different approach.

We're told to come back a few days later to take some more measurements: among other things they weren't able to measure the brain and the heart, because of the position of the baby. What we don't realise at this point, is that our appointment is in a unit specialising in difficult pregnancies. Baptiste and I are aware that the atmosphere shifts, without being able to understand what's really happening. We have a mixed weekend of both questions and reassurances: we think everything will be okay and that perhaps we misunderstood what was said to us. Our friends and family also reassure us, saying that it's likely just a miscalculation of weeks and that everything will be alright. And so, we hope to have good news the following Monday.

During this time, we choose our daughter's name. We feel like she's a child full of joy, that she's bubbly. The name naturally fits these characteristics: our daughter will be called Juliette.

So, we come back into the unit, on Monday morning, without really knowing what is waiting for us. The ultrasound happens in silence. The sonographer is joined by two interns who monitor each image closely. I notice that they are taking more measurements than usual and that they have an abnormal interest in the heart and brain. Once the ultrasound is done, no one says a thing. The doctor settles us in a quiet room and explains that she is going to consult her team to discuss the findings, and then she will come back to share her observations. She has a closed and solemn face. Baptiste and I understand that something serious is happening, but we still don't know quite what. I can't hold back the tears and a feeling of anxiety fills us both. When the practitioner eventually comes back, we feel her worry and that of the two people with her. The specialist does all she can to explain things with gentleness and empathy. She explains that Juliette has serious problems. The list seems unending: the heart has a hole in it, certain areas of the brain aren't developing, her hands and feet are curled up, her trachea is probably not linked to her stomach… None of her organs are working properly. At each spoken word, I feel like a new hatch is opening under my feet and that I'm sinking further and further into the depths of the earth. We want it all to stop but the list goes on and on.

Like a world that crumbles and falls apart, we start to feel like the future cannot be bright under these conditions.

During this meeting, the doctor explains that the team can see that there are serious malfunctions in the child but that at this stage, it is difficult to give a precise diagnosis. The only solution is to have an amniocentesis.[2] The doctor explains that we can do this now or later,

---

2 Amniocentesis is a medical procedure where a sample of amniotic fluid is taken (the fluid which the foetus floats in during pregnancy). The sample is taken through the mother's tummy, through a syringe with a very thin needle.

whichever I prefer. Almost numbed by the impact of this news, I discuss it with Baptiste, and we decide to have the amniocentesis straight away. We want to know exactly what is going on so that we can be prepared, and be fully informed, without there being any grey areas. During the procedure, I feel like the doctor is pushing a sword through my tummy whilst the needle goes in. It is an intrusive and violent sensation.

At that point, I fairly quickly absorbed the fact that the doctor's words were our reality. At the same time, something in me still hoped that someone would come and tell me that no, they were wrong and that everything was fine.

Finally, two days later, we are given a precise diagnosis: Juliette has trisomy 13, a severe chromosomal anomaly. Her chances of survival after birth are minimal. The condition affects her vital organs, so they are not developing properly. If she lives, it will only be for a few hours, a few days, maybe even a few months, but she won't get to her first birthday. Words are not enough to express how we feel at that moment. I feel like an internal explosion mixed with a foggy kind of shock. Just now I want press stop on this situation, like on a tv remote, to not have to face this! And yet I need to, for her and for us.

Once the diagnosis was given, I was tempted to go and do some online research to get an idea of what we would face. If I were to give one piece of advice, it would be to not do this! As soon as I entered 'trisomy 13' into the search bar, photos appeared of the worst cases of trisomy 13: a child with a thumb on its forehead, or with only one eye, six fingers. On top of the shock of the diagnosis, I now had the worry of discovering my daughter's face and body. The photos I saw on the internet left me with the image of a deformed new-born, which led to a real panic inside of me.

Even so, I chose to trust and believe that our first meeting would be gentle, without additional unwanted surprises. The following scans came and confirmed this hope, Juliette's body looked as normal as any new-born.

The medical team explained the options that lay before us. Whatever we decided to do, they were committed to being by our side. There was no doubt in our minds that we wanted to keep her: she was our daughter; we would love her and welcome her as she was. When we told them of our choice, the members of the team expressed their profound respect and assured us of their support. This particular team would be with us all the way through, right until the end, even though my pregnancy had taken on a completely different perspective.

I have immense gratitude for the members of this medical team, for their gentleness, their empathy and their humanity. Every month, we came to see how Juliette was developing and at each appointment, they managed to find the words and the comfort that were needed. They also encouraged us to look ahead, to think about her birth and how we wanted it to happen. They let us express our desires, our dreams for our daughter, all of this whilst being intentionally considerate of our feelings. For example, we had mentioned that we wanted to see our daughter in 3D. We were having monthly sonograms to keep track of Juliette's developments. Whilst we were having one of these 'normal' ultrasounds, the doctor, without warning, changed the probe with another one. The face of my daughter suddenly appeared on the 3D screen. Oh, the emotion! She was perfect, not a trace of any issues. Her little nose, her mouth, her eyes, everything was there, and she was cute as well!

I am all the more in admiration because this is a unit which has complete knowledge of the different outcomes of such a severe trisomy, and yet that didn't stop them from treating our daughter's life with respect, like calling her by her name and underlining her progress.

The news of the diagnosis was certainly a shock for us, but from the very first week, we experienced supernatural peace and joy. We were not devastated. We felt surrounded and supported by heaven. This state of mind may sound unbelievable, given the circumstances, and yet, it's what we experienced, all the way through the pregnancy and beyond.

Our closest friends and family were aware of our situation and worried about it, while we were in a bubble, in the shelter from the storm, and in a place of profound confidence. A seeming paradox given we couldn't control a single thing.

We were measuring the responsibility entrusted to us through the attention we gave Juliette. We rejoiced in the life that was there, conscious that we would experience something special. This joy of knowing that Juliette exists has never really left us.

The progress of the pregnancy

I didn't want to do things differently in how I lived out my pregnancy with Juliette. I lived it in the same fulness as I did with Raphaël, listening to her movements and reactions. In the warmth of her mother's womb, Juliette was not conscious of being sick. She was growing peacefully, knowing she was loved by her family and her Creator. In the end, that was what mattered most to me. Juliette's life came first, and her illness second.

As with Raphaël, from four months into the pregacy, we practiced *haptonomie* to build a connection with Juliette by touching my tummy. She was very responsive and recognised our presence, without a shadow of a doubt.

Over the final weeks, she was even a champion at kicks and somersaults!

Intentionally listening to this growing child, we could see how active and full of life Juliette was. Music woke her up. When Raphaël sang her songs, she would give little kicks, as if to let her big brother know that she liked it a lot. She also responded whenever Baptiste said her name and spoke to her.

Many of us could see how bubbly she was and how she was gifted with a tangible joy. One of our friends noticed that she was very sensitive to candlelight. So, I put this observation into action by regularly taking a bath with Juliette, the room lit up only by candles. These were special moments, where Juliette moved differently and seemed to catch something of the softness and warmth of that light.

After the diagnosis was given, we went to an ultrasound appointment every month. Otherwise, my life went on without any noticeable changes. Every day, I took Raphaël to our activities in various kids' groups, gym classes and music classes. It was important for me that we continued to live in joy, especially allowing Raphaël to flourish. So, I kept going, aware of our reality whilst still welcoming life in all it had to bring.

I wasn't worried during the pregnancy, because I quickly knew that Juliette's life had meaning and that the length of it would not change that. I was with my daughter until the end. There were no moments of profound sadness with her. Even in the moments when I was crying because the circumstances were sad, these were tears with God and the sadness did not last long. God was there with me! I felt completely free to identify my emotions, which were legitimate and to experience them, whatever they were. By welcoming the pain, it went through me without anchoring itself in me. I didn't look for a filter, I simply allowed myself to welcome them, as they came. I noticed that when holding back my emotions and denying them, I suffered much more than when I listened to and peacefully expressed them. I chose to embrace them without dwelling on them, which meant I avoided building a shell around them. One of the keys for me was to be honest with myself. I decided not to stay focused on what was going wrong and to look at the positives. In the end, each day we experienced joy, and each day we went through difficulties, and we had to pick up new challenges. What were we choosing to look at and to live through? Being victims and burying ourselves in suffering? Or giving ourselves to our Creator, confident of His work in our lives?

We also lived life to the full with Juliette. As my pregnancy caused no issues for me, and the doctors saw no reason for extra precautions, amongst other things I kept up cycling until a few weeks before the birth. In April, five weeks before the birth, in the blazing sunshine, we had a memorable bike ride along the coast and in the Scottish isles. I remember the joy of being together, the lightness of everything around us, our laughs, the startling beauty of nature. We were living outside of time, apart from the reality which was waiting for us. It was a real gift! We were full of joy, embracing the life that was there, and we could tell that Juliette grasped this spontaneity. Without knowing it, we were strengthened for the weeks that would come. The timing and circumstances were perfect, made to measure and prepared so that our hearts wouldn't be anchored in sadness.

Baptiste and I have made a habit of sharing every night, before we go to sleep, what we are thankful for that day. This habit has built a heart in us that is predisposed to give *thanks*, no matter what the circumstances are. That's why, even when the diagnosis was given, we were still able to welcome life, *in spite of everything.* Every evening, we kept on sharing what we were grateful for. Not a day went by without us taking stock of the blessings we had received. I think that it is in this habit of thankfulness that we drew the strength to move forward and rejoice in God, despite the difficulties. I also think that thankfulness chases away despair and encourages faith.

Deep down inside of me, I held onto hope for a healing. I longed to see Juliette alive and to hear her baby gurgles. Each ultrasound was both stressful, with the fear that we would be given more bad news, but also carried the joy of seeing Juliette on screen again and the hope of hearing of some improvements. At the 30-week scan, we had an extraordinary breakthrough. While the previous ultrasound had shown a hole in the heart and the trachea that wasn't connected to the stomach, these two problems had disappeared. For us it was more than encouraging, it was a miracle! We started to believe that maybe Juliette would live after all and that maybe she would even be healthy. I felt like wings were pushing me and that the big black cloud from previous weeks was fading away before me. Such joy to think how extraordinary it would be for her to be healed... It was as though we were brushing up to an almost unthinkable miracle and yet something which it seemed could actually happen.

The development of a birth plan

One of the members of our local church, and then the staff of the hospital, told us about C.H.A.S. (Children's Hospices Across Scotland). There are two in Scotland, Robin House and Rachel House, whose vision is to welcome and support children who are at the end of their lives and to support their families. This charity relies on donations and sponsorship.

The specialised unit suggested we write a birth plan from six months into the pregnancy. At this stage, the C.H.A.S. team was integrated into the team that had been following the pregnancy until that point. So, it was with them that we wrote the birth plan. By our side, these professionals encouraged us to think about every possible outcome and to decide how we wanted to face them. Throughout the ultrasounds, several problems were detected and so, at Juliette's birth, we had to be ready to quickly make some vital decisions. The support team always showed such consideration, making us feel fully involved in every step.

If Juliette were to die during the pregnancy, how would the birth take place: by caesarean or vaginally? Would a photographer come to the maternity unit or later at Robin House? At what point would we decide to go to Robin House?

If Juliette were to live after the birth, here's what we could expect: she is born alive but isn't strong enough to survive a surgical intervention. Without an operation, she cannot eat, and her heart is too weak. In this case, nothing could be done to help; but we would spend time with her at the maternity unit, cuddling her until she would leave us. The thought of seeing her die in our arms made me cry every time. I couldn't imagine letting her die without being able to do anything. It was too hard for my mummy heart. It was, however, still a possibility.

On the other hand, if Juliette has enough strength to live and could face surgery, we would have to decide what sort of intervention we want her to have and the consequences these could have on her life.

We couldn't decide anything before the birth, but we could at least express what we didn't want. We specifically decided against aggressive treatments. Given that her life would be brief anyway, then we would choose comfortable interventions that wouldn't cause her any suffering.

Without spreading fear, the team brought up every possible outcome, explaining the physical and moral consequences for Juliette and for us, so that we could face this stage in the best possible way armed with all the facts. Nothing was set in stone in this thought-through process. At any point we could change our minds and make a different decision. The doctors and supporters were by our side ready to adapt. Knowing this brought relief and a feeling of great freedom.

Several weeks later, we went to visit Robin House. On the first floor there are specialised rooms for children needing extra treatment. If Juliette lived, we would sleep there with her. If Juliette died, we could also stay in this house as a family until her burial. During this visit, we found out about the '*Rainbow Room*': a cold room transformed into a child's bedroom, made specially to welcome children who have just died.

As I was pregnant at the time of the visit, even mentioning this possibility was hard for me; but, several months later, this place would be an important part of my journey and restoration.

I found it hard thinking of all the options without knowing which one was waiting for us. Each one of these perspectives brought its load of suffering, without us being able to change it. Everything felt like it was hanging by a thread… Yet, because of this preparation, once we knew the outcome, we would know where to concentrate our efforts and how to deal with the events.

The end of pregnancy and childbirth

On the final stretch of pregnancy, every day of feeling Juliette move was a victory. I counted the days and the weeks, imagining that we might see her alive, maybe even partially or fully healed. The more the days went by, the more my hope grew. My difficult pregnancy, because of the diagnosis, became normal to me as I approached full term.

However, at thirty-six weeks, I realised that Juliette was not moving as she usually did. Where she used to give regular kicks back, she didn't respond. Even when pressing down on my tummy, I could feel her body, but she didn't move. Baptiste and I went to the maternity unit to find out what was happening. But it's a Sunday, and our usual team isn't there. So it's people who don't know our file who examine Juliette. The monitor indicated that her heart was still beating. The midwife told us she couldn't see anything abnormal and sent us home. I was reassured to have seen Juliette's heart beating. Baptiste, on the other hand, was worried that they didn't do any extra tests, given our daughter's situation.

At this point, Baptiste decided to order a car seat and pram set to welcome Juliette alive. This just highlighted the firm hope that we had together of getting to spend time with our daughter once she was born.

In the end, we went back to the maternity unit a few days later for our monthly ultrasound. This time we were in our usual unit, for our monthly check-up. They started the ultrasound. The image on the screen was still, we could not see any movement, not even of the heart. We could all see the same thing from every angle. A few seconds later, the doctor turned to us and said, "I'm sorry…" Juliette's heart has stopped beating and mine stops for a moment as I take in this news. This was it, it was over.

Our hopes to see her alive were swept away in an instant. I came out of this ultrasound room trying to stick together pieces of a puzzle, which had just fallen apart before me. How was this possible, given all the encouragements we were given? Was this really the end, or would there be a dramatic turn of events? My hope tried to stay alive, while my daughter's body was lifeless…

So, we were there, in this hospital, listening to the doctor and the midwife explaining what the next steps would be. I would have to give birth to my lifeless child and, to make the labour easier, I was going to be given a hormone to take and then come back in two days to get labour going. For me, giving birth naturally is a choice and so I didn't want labour to be 'induced' artificially, as I know that can increase the pain. I didn't want to add pain to what is already painful. I get advice about all the possible methods to get this labour going naturally. A friend joined us in the afternoon, and we started making a list of all the things which could help get labour get going, old wives' tales and all! The following day turned into a marathon to get to this goal; included in the program was cycling on cobbled streets!

During this preparation, I was regularly reminding myself that this was a moment I had to go through, it had a time limit, and then another chapter would open; knowing that the story wouldn't end there but that going through this was inevitable, helped a lot. I was at peace, knowing I was signing up for this but that it had its time limit. Aware of this, I knew that I would not fall apart because there would be an 'after'. I also remembered Raphaël's birth, how serene and happy I was at that time. If I managed it without pain for one, I could do it for the other. To lean on what had worked before gave me strength. I prepared for it mentally as though I was running an endurance test. One step after another, one contraction after another, without worrying about the next part, fully anchored in the present moment. At every step, I had to fully trust in my body, in God and in life.

Our prayers and the thousand and one old wives' tales worked, because, on Friday evening, I started having contractions that became stronger. I called the nanny so she could sleep at the house and be there for Raphaël the following morning. At 1.30 am my waters broke. We went to the maternity unit. The specialised unit took us in. Everyone expressed profound respect for our situation. Their support was unwavering, allowing us to go through this challenge in the best conditions. With Baptiste, we were set up in a private room, like a small hotel room, with low light and welcoming atmosphere, just like at home. The medical team had not forgotten any of the details we spoke about in our birth plan. We put worship music on, and I kept the contraction tracker nearby.

The medical staff left us to it and said they would be back to check on progress at 7 am. Hearing that, I looked at Baptiste and told him I would give birth before that. I was right: our little Juliette was born at 6.34 am, without anaesthetic, nor any intervention. During labour, I didn't feel any proper physical pain. I would say it was more 'intensity' than pain. It was so natural and peaceful that we stayed together, just Baptiste and I, without any medical staff right until I could feel that Juliette's head was engaged. The obstetrician could not get over the speed and ease of this labour.

It was during this labour that I grasped a new depth of the sacrifice of Jesus on the cross. In carrying the sufferings of humanity, He joined me in the suffering I went through specifically. I felt a tangible presence and I gave each of my specific physical sensations and emotional sufferings over to Jesus by visualising them on the cross. I also took the step of giving everything that was dead inside of me over to Him, everything that wasn't bearing fruit in my life. Through His cross and resurrection, I knew that He could give me life and transform what wasn't working anymore.

I felt like I was living every aspect of this birth with Him, through what He had done for us. The road that He opened up particularly reflected my situation at that time. This whole journey we had gone on with Juliette, we had walked with Jesus, and I knew deep down how much He was by our side in our family, faithfully, tirelessly.

I knew that Juliette had a destiny to live, and this was established at the start of her conception. So, I also knew that Jesus was not going to abandon us in this crucial moment and that He would look after each of us.

These moments were extraordinary. The sadness was there, as we knew we were giving birth to a stillborn child and at the same time, the presence of heaven was manifest and comforting. The reality of Juliette's personality and the importance of this moment were evident. It was not just a question of 'getting this lifeless body out' and then turning a page. It was about going from being a pregnant woman to meeting our child. Finally, we could meet her, hold her, discover the lines of her face, touch her skin, smell her. We still hold very tender memories of these moments, which I think is in and of itself a miracle!

Living in the present

Since the day of the diagnosis, we were fully aware of how serious the circumstances were, knowing all the possible outcomes we could go through with Juliette. However, we also chose to stay positive, hoping for the best for her and for our family. We moved forward step-by-step, listening to the Creator, to our daughter, and to the doctors. We lived out what it means to 'live in the present'. As soon as we thought about the future in all its possible outcomes, we wavered in sadness and discouragement. As soon as we placed ourselves back in the present, we found God, His promises, and His life. God is in the present, not in the past or the future. That is where He meets us, where He gives us the ability to face things head-on, to live what needs to be lived, and to enter into His plan.

(Baptiste adds: *We went through an experience similar to that of the apostle Peter walking on water. This miracle was able to happen as long as Peter kept his eyes fixed on Jesus, the Creator, and source of the extraordinary in his life. Our perspective of the past, the present, and the future has been enriched and feeds our day-to-day lives.*)

I understood that whenever I leant toward the past or the future, God went quiet, until I came back to His presence. As soon as Baptiste and I contemplated the future with Juliette, we completely lost our footing and were no longer connecting with God. The future was hazardous and destructive, the present was full of life. Juliette was well and truly alive and active in my tummy. It was in positioning my heart in this way that we were able to see who our child was.

Living in this dynamic was a way of life, a discipline to adopt, like that of a high-level sports person training day after day to attain his goal. It is a real challenge to make the choice of joy, to take up this challenge. It was a difficult position to hold onto when faced with certain people who ended up only holding onto the sadness of the context and reminding us of it.

One did not stop the other. We were fully aware that we would definitely lose Juliette sooner or later, but from there we made a choice to look to God and to hold onto the smallest of treasures in our everyday. That's how it was possible to hear Him speak to our hearts and to find the peace and the joy in Him which carried us throughout this challenge.

We also did not have the emotional resources to face the future, because we did not know which tools God would give us to face it when the time would come. We couldn't have known what graces the Lord would bring, equipping us with what we needed every day in order to bring solutions at the right time. That's what helped us not to worry about tomorrow, just as the Gospel invites us to do. That's where we had access to the resources of joy, peace and love. Even the possibility of a miracle in the future didn't fill my thoughts in the present. I was welcoming what was coming, holding onto God to see how He would walk through it by my side.

By staying in the present, the fear of the future melts away. Fear of missing out no longer has a hold and leaves room for confidence.

We would all like to choose what's going to happen in life and yet, certain situations surprise us as is the case with a diagnosis of trisomy 13. We are scared of what we imagine as possible scenarios, scenarios which in the end never come. We are scared because we forget that the resources come in order to support the challenge. Even when what we were scared of actually happens, we realise that it's far less terrifying and destructive than what we had projected.

(Baptiste adds: *Faith is synonymous with trust; it doesn't control circumstances. It's God's choice to reveal Himself in one way or another way. Our hearts were very conscious of this.*)

Trust anchors my soul in peace, whatever adversity I face, whatever the challenges are. Trusting God when He says "yes", when He says "no" or when He says, "not yet". Every day, the Word reminds us that it is good to trust, to lean into the promise that God is faithful and does not let go of our hand. So, it does not matter what pile of worries lies before us. It is interesting to note that "don't be afraid" is quoted three hundred and sixty-five times in the Bible.

For Juliette, I chose to not be afraid, hearing the diagnosis with courage and choosing to face it. Not fearing the medical unit but choosing to team up with them to come out of this having grown. Not being scared to see death face-to-face and to carry this little lifeless body. Not shying away from asking God my questions and listening to His answers.

Staying in a posture of trust and faith, also means not being scared to go through bereavement, to really feel the emotions associated with it, emotions which can sometimes leave you feeling out of control.

In looking for God, our outlook was transformed. From a purely human point of view, we saw a little girl who was seriously ill with not much chance of surviving after birth, but in reality, we saw a little girl, bubbly and full of life, whose final destination was to be in full health, dancing close to the Creator.

Joy in every circumstance

There is joy in tears, hope in mourning, light in the darkness. It is through Juliette that I fully learned this.

At our wedding, Baptiste and I chose Psalm 13.6: "But I have trusted in your steadfast love; my heart shall rejoice in your salvation. I will sing to the Lord because He has dealt bountifully with me." This verse which, from the very beginning, illustrated our hearts' position as a couple, is engraved on our wedding rings. This verse has taken on a whole new meaning and depth in our family since Juliette.

From the beginning of this journey, we felt hope and this perspective stayed written in our hearts: as the saying goes "as long as there is life, there is hope". That's precisely what we experienced with Juliette. Whatever the prognosis and whatever the dark future we could see ahead, as long as she was moving, life was there and there was nothing else to feel.

We discovered that happiness is accessible even through great difficulties, just as people like Nelson Mandela or Corrie Ten Boom[3] have shared, during extreme situations of imprisonment. I do not think that happiness grows instantaneously; it is the result of a choice, of an effort and a personal investment. We learned to cultivate it. In the case of Juliette, we could have dwelt on the situation. It was certainly sad, and we could have fed off this sadness. Instead, we wanted to rejoice in Juliette's life, which was well and truly there, in the midst of us. We decided to trust God and believe that "all things work out for the good of those who love Him" (Romans 8.28). We walked on, along that path, step-by-step, day after day.

At each ultrasound scan, while we listened to the doctor's evaluation and analysis, fully conscious of what was to come, we allowed these two facets to cohabit: the health of our little girl with all the very negative perspectives, and the joy that we felt for her current life. This joy lived in us from the very first week, like

---

3 Corrie ten Boom (Cornelia Johanna Arnalda ten Boom), born on 15th April 1892 in Amsterdam and died on the 15th April 1983 in Orange (California), was a Dutch Christian who helped many Jews escape from the Nazis during World War II. Reportedly, all her family were arrested and sent to a concentration camp. Corrie was the only survivor. After the war, she devoted herself Completely to evangelism. She preached forgiveness through Christ, first in 1946 in Germany and later in over 60 countries all over the world. She put this forgiveness into practice when, in 1947, she met one of the worst camp guardians face-to-face. Corrie wrote a series of Christian books which have been read by many. Her life was the inspiration for the novel *The Hiding-Place* (1971) (La cachette) which was later made into a film.

an extraordinary gift that we learned to cultivate at every stage. Our ultrasound check-ups were actually quite epic! The doctors and nurses who were following us seemed insecure to see us smiling. In order to make sure that we weren't lost in the explanations and in complete denial, they insisted at each appointment on pointing out in detail, all the different aspects of the condition. It was a bit stressful. I remember coming out of one appointment and saying to Baptiste, "I get the impression Juliette has the worst case of trisomy 13 there ever was!" Joy in circumstances like these is sometimes incomprehensible, almost unnatural.

Juliette has a complete place in our family. There's a memory of her written in our lives and this comes out in the words we use when we speak of her, even now.

The moment when her death was announced, we obviously felt sadness – like a blade – but we also felt joy. The joy of knowing she was with God, that we would meet her again someday. Having this joy doesn't take any of the pain away, the loss of living without her, but it gives a perspective which isn't limited to the present situation. The pain fades, the joy remains.

Raphaël's transformation

Not long after the diagnosis, we chose to talk to Raphaël about the situation. We had already told him a few weeks earlier that he was going to be a big brother. So, it seemed obvious that he should know what was really going on.

We told him using simple words, explaining that Juliette, his little sister, was very sick and that we did not know if he would get to know her, but that she would be his little sister, whatever happened. We also had it on our hearts to set him free from our own emotions. We didn't want him to carry things, which weren't his to bear. We wanted him to live what he was going to live, without feeling weighed down by his parents' emotions. So, we told him that if he felt we were sad or preoccupied, it wasn't his fault and we wanted him to be free to feel his own emotions. He listened to us at only 20 months old, concentrating as well as he could at that age; then, once he had taken the situation in, he went off to play with his little cars. It was as simple as that.

As soon as we created a welcoming environment for our emotions, we were each free to feel and express them.

Raphaël gave kisses and hugs to Juliette in my tummy, throughout the pregnancy. It was very clear to him that a little person was developing and that he could interact with her. Children grasp sickness and death simply and without it being a taboo subject.

We, therefore, lived our relationship with Juliette to the full, making the most of the present moment, each moment she was living and interacting with us. As we described the situation very simply to Raphaël, it was then easy, when the time came, to explain that Juliette had died and that she was now living with Jesus. The medical team who were alongside us encouraged us to use real words, to describe the situation as it was. Children don't dread death as we do. Telling him that Juliette flew off to heaven or that she went away (a blurry notion) only creates confusion. We wanted to avoid that.

Juliette was a carrier of joy, and we believe that Raphaël received an extra dose of that through her. During the pregnancy, we saw him grow in this area. He was rather serious before Juliette, not sad but serious, yet he began expressing more and more joyfulness. Even on the day of Juliette's death, we felt he was different, as though she had left him this gift of joy: pure, crystal radiant. He could have been worried to not see us when he woke up, as we had left for the maternity ward, but he was happy, laughing in his bed and showing no signs of worry in our absence. The nanny was surprised by this. After this, he was very present in all we were going through, all the while with a lightness that children carry at his age.

A few months after Juliette's passing, I was chatting to Raphaël. He was showing me some sun cream and telling me that it was for the baby. While explaining to him that this was also for him, he replied, "No mummy, it's for the baby." Seeing his insistence, I asked him which baby he was talking about. To that he replied, "Well, you know, Mummy and Daddy's baby!" I kept going. "Do you mean Juliette?" To this question, he exploded with joy, clapping his hands and exclaiming, "Yes! Juliette, Juliette, Julieeeeette." I realised at that moment how Raphaël had both fully grasped the situation, and that he had also absorbed the joy that she carried. I was gobsmacked, emotional and touched.

The ceremony in honour of Juliette's life

We chose to prepare a ceremony to celebrate Juliette's life and honour all the fruits that her short life on earth had produced. We wanted to meet in a church building that was close to where we lived so that our neighbours and friends could join us. More than 70 people came, even though we had only been in the country for 7 months…

In the church, we asked for festive decorations, with balloons like ones you would find at a kid's party. We invited everyone who came to come dressed colourfully, rather than being dressed for mourning. To allow everyone to express themselves, we also suggested they bring or send us artistic creations linked with how Juliette inspired them. This allowed friends further away to take part in the celebration. Baptiste and I were aware that, given the circumstances and the geographic distance, it was not only difficult to travel but also to find the right words and attitudes to support us. That's also why we suggested contributions through art. A space was set up for this with photos, texts, poems, children and adults' drawings, which reflected the character of our little Juliette, joyous and full of life.

A path of candles was laid out to remember Juliette's sensitivity to candles and her bubbly character. Throughout the ceremony, we spoke of her, sang, prayed, and cried.

Baptiste and I prepared the order of service and wrote several texts which we read. It was also important for us to say what we were grateful for. As an introduction to the song 'Miracle',[4] which proclaims that God is the God of miracles, we said this:

"Today we are:
- Sad but not devastated,
- struck down but not overcome[5],
- disappointed, but we haven't lost hope,
- torn, but full of joy to one day find her again in heaven and healed.

Despite the sadness and questions, we believe that God remains the same."

During the ceremony, our community and the team from Robin House were by our sides and made sure their support was felt in all the little details. Two couples,

---

4   'Miracle' *Let it Echo*, Chris Quilala (2016).

5   2 Corinthians 4:7-10: *"But we have this treasure in jars of clay, to show that the surpassing power belongs to God and not to us. 8 We are afflicted in every way, but not crushed; perplexed, but not driven to despair; 9 persecuted, but not forsaken; struck down, but not destroyed; 10 always carrying in the body the death of Jesus, so that the life of Jesus may also be manifested in our bodies."*

friends of ours who supported us throughout this journey, sat to our left and our right, all holding us tightly. A person from C.H.A.S was available to look after Raphaël when it was needed. Our words in French were translated into English. And our families and friends from France then also had a translation from English to French.

After the ceremony, a wonderful buffet of cakes, teas, and coffees was carefully prepared. We stayed in the church a long time chatting with one another. Each person also took the time to look at the artistic corner, to read the texts, and see the images on display, so as to absorb the shock of the event. All this was organised in a few days, in a movement of extraordinary solidarity which we are profoundly grateful for.

Several people told us that the ceremony had overwhelmed them. They were able to witness that it is possible to convert the worst events into joy, to a message of hope, and to draw a supernatural strength from it. Juliette transmitted this heritage with strength: joy whatever the circumstances.

The people who lived alongside us during the pregnancy speak of Juliette as though they have met her, with bright eyes and a smile on their faces. This life and joy have continued to live in us since her passing. To me, it is a magnificent heritage, which Juliette has left to us.

A supportive environment

Support from the medical team

The medical team displayed unwavering support throughout. The kindness and attention we found on every level is one of the things that surprised me most about living in Scotland.

Each one of the doctors or nurses who accompanied us was able to be thoughtful and concerned about our wellbeing. They used their words delicately when speaking with us, taking time to address questions at every stage. Knowing we were sincerely listened to and taken seriously in our decisions made a big difference. I have immense gratitude for the hospital staff.

At the maternity unit on the night of the birth, after the medical care and once Juliette was placed in her bassinet, Baptiste went home. He joined Raphaël and tried to rest after a night without sleep. The nurses encouraged me to sleep a bit. I must have slept for an hour then I woke up. My first thought was to go and see my daughter in her bed. Deep down I knew that she was lifeless, but I surreptitiously felt the pure joy of looking to see my child after having slept. Seeing her motionless broke my heart and I broke down in tears, curled up in my bed. Waves of grief kept coming over me.

I hadn't heard the door open: a nurse was coming to comfort me. She found just the right words in such a painful moment. She sat at the edge of my bed and first she told me how beautiful Juliette was. She spoke about my daughter as though she was alive. Then she welcomed my hurt, telling me it was painful, and it would take time to recover. She opened me up to a happier perspective, helping me realise that I would lift my head but that it would happen gradually. She didn't try to give me empty words. She was able to be authentic and realistic while helping me see beyond this imposing mountain of grief before me. She helped me to reconnect with the present and to the joy of being a mother. I felt heard and honoured.

This woman played an essential role. She came to stretch out her hand without fear. I couldn't tell you who she was, I don't even know her name, but her intervention has stayed engraved on my heart.

Life at Robin House (C.H.A.S.)

We were welcomed into Robin House just after Juliette's birth until her cremation.

The children's hospice is located in the green surroundings of a loch. The families are taken care of entirely, housed in private rooms. Cooks prepare our meals each day. All the families living in the house at that moment eat at the same table. There was such a respect for one another's intimacy that we felt free to stay in our bubble or to start a conversation with our neighbours, without forcing anything. One of the team members was dedicated to each of the families there. She was there to listen to and support us. A chaplain was also there to help us in the administrative procedures: reporting her death, taking care of her coffin, preparing the funeral. The moral support of the personnel was so very helpful. The accompanying person (who changes depending on shifts), came and introduced herself in the morning then disappeared, whilst letting us know that she was there, if we needed her.

C.H.A.S's approach is to listen to the families. It isn't the families who have to adapt to the structure, but the teams who adapt to people's needs. It is one thing to claim this, but we can truly attest to it in this establishment. There was not one moment when anything was imposed on us or where we felt misunderstood with regard to what we were feeling. Thanks to this respectful support delivered with such gentleness, we were able to bring up questions step-by-step, whilst being guided and carried in the decisions we made.

C.H.A.S.'s vision is to allow children to live the best moments of their life, whatever its length may be. Joy is the motto of these establishments. This applies to the sick children as well as their brothers and sisters. The architectural layout means there are spaces dedicated to children's lives: a games room, a music room, a sensory room, a soft play area, a heated pool, outdoor play areas, dens… The team suggests entertainment for the children. There are regular visits during the week from music therapists, giant soft toys, clowns, singers…

Raphaël loved his stay. A year later, he still speaks of it excitedly remembering all of the playful areas of the house!

C.H.A.S. show tenderness in looking to create memories for the parents and surviving children. The team did this generously, and one way it did this was to offer us a box of souvenirs with different objects reminding us of our daughter. The person in charge of manual and artistic activities came and took Juliette's feet and handprints. We have wonderful coloured paintings of her pretty little feet and hands so perfectly formed. One of these paintings is a canvas of our family with each of our prints and with space for other children to come. The personnel team made sure we lived out the grieving process in the gentlest way possible. They also helped us to see further and to make out a future which was difficult to see clearly, but no detail was amiss.

The Rainbow Room is laid out and decorated like a child's nursery. The body of the child dressed and swaddled in covers is placed in a pretty basket. Our little Juliette stayed in this room from the day she was born until her cremation ten days later.

We were able to see and carry Juliette in our arms for four days then she was placed in her coffin. These moments with her stay engraved in the depths of my heart. At first it was hard for me to touch her, I was scared to damage her. The accompanying person explained that there was no risk to hold her in my arms and she encouraged me to do so. I came to see Juliette many times and little-by-little I got to know this lifeless body. Carrying and talking to her helped me take in what I was going through. I was able to give words to the dull pain and incomprehension. It was also in these intimate moments that I poured out my heart to God and that I begged Him for this to bring fruit in my life.

Four days later, a person from the funeral-home came to place Juliette in the coffin we had chosen. The lid stayed open for another two days and we were there when they closed it.

On the first day, a professional photographer came to offer us a photoshoot with her. A few days later he had prepared a "special gift for a special family" (his words): a box with many edited and printed photos. On one of them, you can see me carrying Juliette and you can see a stuffed elephant at the front of the photo, "Because an elephant never forgets," explained the photographer, his eyes full of emotion. It was very touching to feel thought of so much and to see that the team valued the smallest details of our daughter's life.

Many professionals offer their services for free to the families staying in Robin House. For instance, the photographer who offered us the photoshoot shared with us that he was at the end of his career and was looking to do something that would feed his soul. In giving us the photos, he explained that taking photos of our little Juliette moved him profoundly and that he felt something special in her presence.

From birth until her cremation, the team around us always made sure that Juliette's body was near us. At the maternity unit, she was placed straight away in a mobile cold cot, next to my bed. Her body was in the car with me when we went to Robin House. We sat by her coffin when we went to the funeral and the cremation. This aspect might seem anecdotal, but it was essential for us and it reflects the gentleness and attention shown to Juliette's existence. The link we had with her was fully respected. At no moment did we have to suffer from anyone's abruptness, or did we feel that she was torn away from us. Their attention came to rest like a soothing balm on the wound of our loss, a balm which would remain.

Looking back, I realised that if we had been in denial of the consequences of Juliette's illness, namely a premature death, we would have spent all our energy trying to change reality, missing out on the time we had to meet her. We probably would have missed out on the resources available to us to get through each stage. C.H.A.S. was a major resource, which made all the difference. Through them, heaven came to our aid in these different circumstances.

And in a way, we can say that this place was prepared in advance for us, in that it already existed when I arrived in Scotland already pregnant, without knowing what was to come. We could have landed anywhere else in the world and not received what we did.

The red robin and its symbolism

The house that welcomed us is called Robin House. Whilst digging into the symbolism of the red robin, I was struck by how it perfectly illustrated our journey with Juliette. The red robin is a bird that sings in the heart of winter. It brings hope, life in the midst of aridity.

In Scotland, he's the symbol of resurrection. The story goes that a red robin was found dead by a certain Mungo who resurrected him.

Juliette was not in fact resurrected here on earth, but she made us understand how real life in heaven is, how it's a new birth, a continuing of our life on earth.

Glasgow's coat of arms[6]

Mural painting – High street in Glasgow – (By SMUG)

In doing some research, two Scottish legends mention this bird and poetically illustrate the symbolic weight of this feathered animal.

---

6   Glasgow's coat of arms refers to the life (or legend) of Saint Mungo, patron saint and founder of the city of Glasgow (in the 6th century). He is represented at the top wearing bishop's clothes. The red robin who he is said to have resurrected is perched on top of the tree. The city motto written underneath is inspired by Saint Mungo's prayer: *"Let Glasgow flourish by the preaching of your Word and the praising of your name."*

First legend

"A long time ago at the beginning of time, little grey birds were full of love, compassion and would happily and fearlessly draw near to humans, on account of their tenderness towards them.

"One day, one of these little birds, seeing a suffering man on a cross, flew around him to comfort him. He wiped the tears of Christ with his wings; with his beak, he tore out the thorns wounding his head, then a drop of blood fell on his neck, colouring his feathers forever.

"This was the blood of Christ. And so, this little bird became red and grey and was henceforth called 'red robin'. Since then, he approaches humans even more to remind them of the martyrdom of Jesus…"

Second legend

"Unto Jesus who was praying in the olive garden, a little bird drew near. High on needle-thin legs, his brownish feathers a little olive, his eyes round like blackcurrants, he passed by skimming the ground, jumping and sometimes stopping to bow. A breeze had told him that this man here was the heart itself become man. What did this little sparrow want then? He wanted to visit the heart of the Son of God. And so, smiling, Jesus opened His heart, and the little bird entered the cage in His ribs: he was taken with love, and beat his wings to the divine rhythms and beats. In memory of this visit, Jesus marked him with the light of His blood on his chest. From then on, the bird was called red robin. Every day, the red robin discreetly bears witness to this legend on the branch of time."[7]

---

7 Henri Pichette, *Les Ditelis du rouge-gorge*, Gallimard, 2005. The 'ditelis' (a word invented by the author) are very brief poems, somewhere between nursery rhymes and sayings, beautiful inventions in language which are also a testimony of his own spiritual search.

The support of our family and friends

We have been touched by the support of our friends and family, whether it be in France, or in Scotland where we came to settle. It was vital to be in a caring environment which healthily welcomed our choice in carrying on a pregnancy where there is a severe disability. This is precisely what we found in Scotland: a friendly and community-centred environment.

Friends from France and other places also supported us. We regularly received little messages, kind attention and prayers. They were by our sides in a tangible way even if, for certain loved ones, the distance was difficult to bear. (If you're reading these lines, rest assured, we knew we were loved by you. Even if you didn't know what to say or how to say it, we knew who our loved ones were and were aware that there wasn't really much to say!) For us, friendships have remained stable, like set cement, whatever winds may blow, the distance doesn't change anything.

I can think of this friend who was pregnant at the same time as me. Throughout the pregnancy, we shared our day-to-day, the joys, the pains and our faith. Seeing her little girl today reminds me of the moments I shared with her mum and makes me imagine what Juliette could have become. Our girls would be days apart in age. Even though the absence of Juliette is there, and we can't change it, the authenticity of our exchanges during this particular time enriched our bond.

For others, the support could be as simple as "I know it's difficult", full of heart and compassion. Simply being taken into someone's arms, as soon as I mentioned my situation, without going into detail, was enough to give me courage to keep going. I was also encouraged by the friends who just cried with me. All these people – old friends as well as newer ones – said little with words, but 'said' a lot through their actions, through a look, through the attention they gave. Through this drama, but also by experiencing other beautiful moments together, our bonds have become particularly strong and solid.

We were profoundly moved by the support we received in Scotland. Our church quickly became a source of sincere and strong friendships. We also connected well with our neighbours, many of whom became friends.

Life here is organised around families and activities for children. Churches in the neighbourhood make their halls available for families. A room is filled with toys for 0 to 3-year olds, and another allows parents to have a cup of tea while keeping an eye on their children. It is possible to go to a new venue every day to meet new people, which makes it easier to build relationships. I had barely arrived in a new place, and I already had made some lasting connections. It's quite natural for me to connect with people, but this set up was a real facilitator. At the time, we didn't know about Juliette's condition, but retrospectively, I can see how much the environment helped in getting us through the challenge we would face.

Among the friends I met here, I particularly remember one who, on the day of the diagnosis, shared with me that she had gone through the same story, seven years earlier. Being at the start of this journey, she was there for me, step-by-step, like a reassuring mirror. She helped me to look further, to keep hoping in life and I am profoundly thankful to her. Since then, our friendship has been solid as a rock!

I also think of two Scottish friends who were faithfully there, on alert for every ultrasound, every medical visit, and were really watching over me. One of them would regularly make a point of asking me how I was feeling. She encouraged me to express my emotions and supported me when I needed it. These questions sometimes pushed me to my limits, but I was able to keep going with this exercise because I felt I could safely share this intimate part of my life with her. I also felt I could choose not to talk if I didn't want to. She was the one who came to support me when I had just found out Juliette had passed away. The other friend came to visit on the Friday night, just before the contractions started!

A pastoral couple in our church also played an important role in supporting us. We could feel that they were solid people, and we could lean on them at any moment. It was reassuring to know that they were by our side. They were the first people to tell us about Robin House. In hindsight, I think that without them, we would maybe have been more reticent to take an interest in this particular facility.

During the pregnancy, our neighbour and two young ladies from the church offered their help with looking after Raphaël whenever we needed it. This practical support was very precious in allowing us to go to our medical appointments.

We also had precious practical support when Juliette passed away, not only from Robin House but also from our local community. A food train was organised between our neighbours and our church friends; the friends from different groups bringing us meals for three weeks after our stay at Robin House. For the whole time, we were helped in quite an incredible way, with practical needs and meals. The company Baptiste works for also offered him two weeks of compassionate leave, even though he'd only been with the company for six months. Some friends all clubbed together to hire us a car for a week, to allow us to have a break away after the ceremony.

While Juliette was in the *Rainbow Room*, we invited several close friends and family to meet her. Our close family, two couples of friends here, and the pastoral couple who were supporting us came. It was painful to introduce them to our lifeless daughter but equally comforting that they could see her, that they witnessed her. What happened in this room, especially with our recent friends, sealed something profound and unique between us. We will never forget these moments we shared together.

A couple of friends made a return trip in 24 hours to be able to attend the funeral. Others came to visit us a few weeks later. Two months after Juliette's passing, we went back to France to see our loved ones who weren't able to travel. Our hearts are so thankful for the loving care they showed us.

There are pains which only cry inside, like elusive sighs, unspeakable. Everyone did what they could, with their own heart, their own baggage and their own sensitivity. Only one word comes to my mind to them all: 'thank you'. Thank you for being there, thank you for your friendship, thank you for your authenticity.

Which words or attitudes were most helpful?

Going through events such as those we experienced sheds light on what we clearly need but also on what really doesn't 'help'. Having experienced this all now, I have a better grasp on what can really destabilise people who are going through it.

Whilst we were at peace and confident, we were confronted with people breaking down at the news of Juliette, and then we had to comfort them. Their sadness, their negativity, came and made our peace more fragile. It was strange being there, us who were closest to this grief, yet expressing what we believed and how grateful we were for this life. Having said that, we did not let ourselves get dragged down by these people, and we actually noticed that this joy, this hope which we carried, was contagious and led many to see the situation from a different perspective.

Even though one's story can awake in another their own pains, it is helpful to feel that we don't have to carry each other, but rather that we can share and support one another in our shared pain.

Other loved ones expressed their worries at us being in a foreign country. And yet we were already well supported. We did not want for anything. We could reassure them all we wanted, but it was hard for them to imagine this cocoon which we were in, and even harder to put into words what was going on in our hearts.

Thankfully, we did not have to deal with the judgement of certain Christians who say or think that such a tragedy is due to hidden sin, or some kind of curse. Like the disciples of Jesus who, in seeing a man who was born blind, asked their master if this condition was due to the unfortunate man's sin or that of his parents (John 9:2). To me, this way of thinking is not Christian (God doesn't avenge our sins through inflicting sorrows). And this 'well meaning' but self-righteous attitude is offensive to people going through immense difficulties.

Even when the unfortunate have sinned, in love God reveals it gently, with compassion and at the right time. Job's[8] friends brought accusations about his life even though in the eyes of God he was beyond reproach. Despite the accusation of his so-called 'friends', Job was able to hold onto his confidence that, with God, he would get through these challenges and would come out having grown. We do not see the full picture of our lives and we

---

8   Job 11:2-6.

can't always explain the 'why' behind certain events, but we must always make room within ourselves for trust.

What helps people facing challenges like these, is not to assume their needs; that creates a feeling of being bogged down and an obligation of thanks which can make the situation even more heavy than it really is. Unless you were to know us perfectly, which would be impossible, assumptions can bring a lot of awkwardness and misunderstanding. It felt natural and legitimate for us to inform our close ones of this journey which we were on. It was really our desire to communicate with everyone around us. Not as a call for help, nor an expectation that any particular help would be given. This is just how we do friendships, without weighing people down, simply taking care of our connection.

And yet, our situation awoke the 'saviour' in certain people. This reaction, which at a first glance may seem touching, very quickly becomes invasive, especially in circumstances where privacy is vital.

On the other hand, other people had a subtle way of being able to anticipate and suggest help which we hadn't yet been able to think of. And they were right! More generally, maybe the most appropriate approach would be simply to say, "I'd like to be there for you. Tell me what I can do to be a support to you." This approach makes us active agents in the process. We then have to learn to express what we need. It can be embarrassing when people think for us and want to do things "for our own good".

And so, naturally, I turned toward certain people around me who, I knew, would have the right words and a good attitude. This didn't exclude others, but, depending on the moment, it brought relief to sometimes be able share closely with just a chosen few.

During and after the pregnancy, I was able to turn towards these relationships that did me good, but at other times, I preferred to have time alone or time for us just as a couple, still aware my close ones weren't far, ready to support me.

I would encourage loved ones not to remind people going through a challenging situation that the situation is difficult, for example, underlining that there is nothing worse than to lose a child. Being the first in line, this information hadn't escaped us! This sort of 'support' isn't that at all; the person expressing this becoming more of a commentator on misery: but to us, it's *our* story.

Reminding someone of the challenge brings discouragement and a profound sense of powerlessness. What is truly precious, on the other hand, is to feel that the person in front of us understands and sympathises with what is happening. The simple fact of knowing that person is truly present, and available to listen, is already very comforting.

Being in a supportive role can sometimes be a subconscious way of running from one's own problems and to feel comforted by thinking, "I'm there for them but thank God I'm not in the same situation!"

This can sometimes be a way of signing up to the role of 'helper', a more comfortable position than that of 'person in need', without having to join in with your own vulnerability. This attitude, even if it isn't spoken, is felt in the way the support is given. It gives the impression that the person is repairing herself through the event or that they have adopted a form of invulnerability, without really stretching out a hand to the other. This translates in the end as a form of condescendence and sentimentality which doesn't help anything, and just highlights the hurt.

I learned to accept and let go, thinking that even if something touches on what I'm going through, what's going on does not belong to me and in the end, it isn't my problem. My position was to stay open and, at some point, to choose to maintain the connection or distance myself. I hoped that maybe, experiencing my vulnerability, others would go on a journey towards more vulnerability themselves.

This perspective brings up lots of questions. Do we need the misery of others to measure our own happiness? Is the misfortune someone has been through actually experienced by them as such? For instance, I have discovered in my travels that some people who are labelled as poor were actually rich in their joy of living and were far from needing pity.

In these moments, I think it's essential to evaluate who has the resources, the understanding or the space to understand and be a support. Everyone goes through their own challenges at different times and it's not always easy to have the capacity to be present. I was comfortable with this idea and wasn't hurt by it. On the contrary, accepting it helped me see more clearly, not to feed high expectations and to surround myself with the right people.

It seems essential to me that the Christian body finds a balance between encouragement through faith and staying anchored in what's real. It's simplistic to proclaim, "God will heal", without leaving room to share what we are feeling, along with our fears and our questions. It can leave us sensing that, for these 'religious' people, this situation has to change, as if not it means that we have a problem with God. It can even become a polite way of policing what the other is saying, implying that they don't want to hear about the real state of the situation; this adds heaviness to an already difficult experience. Sometimes, we can run after an instantaneous change, when there's actually a maturing in the process of living out the challenge we are facing. It seems to me that this second part of the journey is just as rich in its teaching and is worth being valued.

And then there are those who have the right response and for us that was the majority of the people we met. They were able to be there, in many different ways, without doing too much, without becoming invasive or insistent. Those who listened without making assumptions, who grasped the severity of the situation, without reminding us how difficult it was. Some were also able to keep their sadness to themselves for a time so they could receive ours. Others, in the end, didn't know quite how to react and so they disappeared, while the storm passed, which was perhaps a less harsh approach. Sometimes it is better to say nothing than to say something unhelpful or insensitive! Actually, some of the silences were charged with a real presence. Silence does not mean indifference.

Now that I've made a list of difficult behaviours, let's take a breath and relax! I know that I have probably said unhelpful or insensitive things to loved ones going through difficult times. We are human, and we do what we can, with all we are and carry.

How we went through this as a couple

Baptiste and I have a different way of approaching events. I can immediately put into words what I'm feeling by talking it through with a listening ear. Baptiste, he is more internal, needing to take time apart without expressing himself. In other words, I verbalise my emotions, while he synthesises it all and then finds just the right soothing phrase to calm the inner storm.

I have learnt through the years not to judge how something works by comparing it to something else. There isn't a good or bad way of working. We are just different and that is what makes us so compatible and our connection so rich. With Juliette, we went through the whole day-by-day reality fully together, whilst feeling things in different ways and at different speeds. And in the end, that's what gave us strength. When one was sad, the other was there to cheer them up and vice-versa. It seemed essential to consider each other's feelings, these sometimes very raw emotions, without letting ourselves be weighed down by what the other was going through. It was equally essential to be united on the decisions we would make and the inner postures we would adopt.

In the darkest moments, simply knowing Baptiste's presence, and able to nestle into his arms and cry, helped me to face what was next. I remember that in the first days at Robin House, I was living in a fog; Baptiste and I were literally exhausted. The first night, I woke up and could not stop sobbing. Baptiste took me in his arms until the shaking stopped and until I could fall asleep again. There was nothing left to say. The grief due to the emptiness left in me by Juliette seemed huge.

We came out of this challenge strengthened, carrying a deeper love for one another and confident in our capacity to confront the crises together, while still taking care of our needs and that of our family. We know we've been trained to handle difficulties without bending, without running from them, confident in our capacity and even more essential, fully assured of God working by our sides.

A time for questions

Where is God in all this?

I have never felt so close to God as I did through this challenge, and I felt His presence all the way through to the end. It was after Juliette's death that I confronted this crucial question: who is this God in whom we have put our trust? Where do we put God in this equation, when suffering is unleashed? God is all-powerful. He is able to heal Juliette. Why is it that a God who is so powerful, who is capable of the impossible, did not intervene to change Juliette's condition?

We say that God is in control, that He is by our sides but that He leaves us free choice. But, practically, it isn't my free will that led me to choose that Juliette would bear a severe disability and die prematurely. The Bible says that God wants the best for our lives but it's inconceivable that the best would lead to this. Honestly, being conscious of the power of God, I would have liked Him to have taken full control of the situation according to my vision of what was best. I don't know if I will get answers to my questions. What I do know is that He maybe didn't accomplish the miracle that we were hoping for, but He was glorified in what happened, without a doubt. I have no doubt either about the love of God for us, of His faithfulness and His infinite goodness.

I went through other questions and internal battles. In the end, who is this God in whom I believe who doesn't stop evil but just gives us the 'strength' to face it? For what purpose? I believe that He is all-powerful, and I know that He is capable of doing big things, but that maybe makes the situation even more difficult to bear. In my case, He let things happen and gave me 'boosts' to get through the challenge; but it didn't take away the visceral suffering that I could feel. To what end? Once we have gotten over this challenge, what will be left? During this season, I wasn't able to imagine how God would be able to use this. I couldn't see past my hurt. With time, new perspectives opened up, and with them peace and transformation came.

Where do I place my trust in God? What can guarantee that no other terrible thing will happen to us? What does it mean to say God protects us? I would like to trust that nothing will ever happen to us, but my experience proves the contrary. And how do we feel reassured after Juliette? I've lost the formula… Even if the grace to face it is there, I am living through a tragedy which should never have happened, in my opinion. I really thought that nothing significant could fall on us. But, in the end, anything dramatic can happen to us… I think it's terrible to build trust in that! How do we do it then? All of these questions were haunting me during the grieving process, without finding real answers. An onslaught of catastrophic scenarios filled my imagination, as though every possible imaginable drama would happen to me some day or another. And gradually, I found the road to confidence, knowing from experience that what I fear most generally doesn't happen to me. And what I don't anticipate can actually happen, but it always comes with resources to live through it.

I had other questions which went through my head after Juliette. In the context of the pregnancy, I had a lot of faith and momentum to pray for the situation to change. I saw changes in my character, my emotions and even in Juliette's development, as was highlighted through the different sonograms. And yet, the end to this pregnancy was death, and through this death my rock of faith had moved. I questioned myself easily: what is the point in praying for a situation to change? God knows the beginning and the end. And in this perspective, where do we play an active role? In Juliette's case, believing for a miracle gave me strength, joy and stamina. Seeing her dead in my arms, I was not angry with God. I simply thought that He knew what He was doing and that He would work through it for the best. But it was afterwards that this question stayed with me. I couldn't bring myself to be cross with God, but I had a hard time understanding and maybe accepting what happened to us. What does it mean then, to know God and to know that He is capable of doing miracles if *these* miracles don't really happen? I was having a sort of internal war in thinking that yes, I can see Him doing things in my life, but I have the impression that these things are like crumbs compared to all His potential.

Believing brings a lot of momentum and allows us to draw from our internal resources. A few months after the loss of Juliette, I felt as though this energy had left me. I was literally emptied of my faith momentum. I still had this trust in God, knowing that He loved me, but it seemed to me that there was a contradiction between being aware of the greatness of God and realising that it wasn't manifesting in the way that I thought it would. I had lost the momentum to go after miracles, healings and profound changes.

I was a little like the disciple Thomas in the gospels[9], I needed to *see* a physical miracle with my own eyes and

9   John 20:24-29.

be captivated by the greatness of God. I wanted to see this God who heals the sick and raises the dead and at the same time, I couldn't help but think that He hadn't done so for my daughter. It was hard to come face-to-face with the definitive aspect of death. I couldn't expect anything and that was painful. Basically, my emotions collided!

For a moment, I even had the impression I was losing my faith, because of my reluctance to pray. Someone reminded me that faith is not only placed in healing but also in the comfort of God. Knowing that we can come and draw comfort in Him and turn to Him when we need to also builds faith. Hearing these words brought relief and helped me to get going again.

When I was pregnant, it annoyed me to hear people say that God cried with me. Either I kept quiet, or I answered that He could do a lot more than just cry about it. And knowing that He was crying made me want to shake Him and to say, "Hey, hey, it's not the time for crying, you need to do something, heal my daughter, she is going to die!" And in the end, this feeling only grew after her death. I told myself that He couldn't do much more than be with me in this trial, and that maybe it wasn't His role to change the laws of nature to suit me. I became a little sceptical about His power, even maybe sarcastic at times. An internal battle began with the feeling that in the end, the God on whom I relied was only a 'small god'. He wasn't an active agent in the details of our lives!

There was this song[10] that I listened to over and over which forged a new path in my heart. This song came and gradually resounded in me and became a prayer.

During all this time of questioning and tiredness, I could see how much Juliette's life did not end with her brief time on earth but that she had an eternity of life in

---

10   Rend collective, *Weep with Me* - Album "Good news".

heaven. Understanding this aspect of Juliette's life led me to absorb it more deeply for myself as well.

Gradually, the storm calmed. I can't say precisely what happened, nor at what point, but I chose to fully put my trust in God, to give Him my hand once again. From what I understand of the all-powerfulness of God, everything is a question of love. At first, I couldn't see the link: how could love make sense of death and the suffering associated with it? Little-by-little, this gentle strength rooted itself in my heart. Love is different to sentimentality. It doesn't depend on circumstances, nor on people. This assurance that love is there, and that it never lets us down was established in me. When I read what I've gone through again, I think that the only thing that really matters is love. At the end of our lives, it's what we will remember; we will think over the years gone by about the love that was manifest in us, and which we were able to share with others. Love can do anything and the God who I know loves us fiercely, faithfully, unconditionally.

And as God is Love, it's natural to turn to Him, whatever is going on. Certain tragedies happen, that's how the world works, but we can lean on God, knowing that through His resurrection power, nothing will remain dead forever. He will compose new music through the suffering in our lives, which resounds through the past, present and future. It's about the love of God first but also the love of ourselves and the love of others.

God's glory is goodness, and this goodness is manifest to mankind in a glorious way. Through Juliette, I have grasped this glorious dimension in a different way, maybe as gentler and more accessible.

Throughout this journey, I was conscious of the way I understood God as all-powerful as being more like the depictions of Greek gods than that of the God in the Bible. Greek gods are efficient warriors, flattening everything in their way, but they lack this heart-to-heart relationship with mankind. They pursue their goal and bring it to pass whatever the cost. The God of the Bible is not only powerful, but also personal, compassionate and full of love. He works alongside us, shapes us, step-by-step, in order to become the person He created. When I think about the love of God for me, I see Him at the centre of huge human masses, pushing through the crowd to make a way without giving up and without ever losing sight of me, to come to my aid. Through His love for us, He will fight until the end and will never abandon His creation.

Going from why to how

Although the possibility of a miracle was conceivable in our faith context, Baptiste and I quickly got to the point of saying: "Who are we to tell God what He should do?" The basis of our faith is that He loves us, that we love Him and that we consecrate our lives to Him so that He can be glorified in us.[11] From this place, confidence flows, and we can move forward, hand-in-hand with Him, expecting the best. Whether we experience 'happiness' or 'misfortune' according to our human concepts, it's always so that He can be glorified, inasmuch as we allow Him to be.

I'm not saying that I don't battle with questions, but this trial has allowed me to come back to a simple and powerful foundation of the reality of the nature of God. I know, internally, that God is basically love, yet I'm

---

11 See 2 Corinthians 3:18 "And we all... beholding the glory of the Lord, are being transformed into the same image from one degree of glory to another. For this comes from the Lord who is the Spirit."

See also 2 Corinthians 4.6-7 "For God, who said, 'Let light shine out of darkness,' has shone in our hearts to give the light of the knowledge of the glory of God in the face of Jesus Christ. But we have this treasure in jars of clay, to show that the surpassing power belongs to God and not to us."

conscious that, in this world, evil exists and that it can manifest itself, even if we have faith.

As Christians, we can quickly imagine that nothing difficult can happen to us, as though Christianity is like a vaccine that makes us 'one hundred percent immune' against the difficulties in life. Jesus never promised us that we would be spared every misfortune; He told us that He would be with us all the days of our lives.[12] That's actually a very different promise! But it is strengthening to know that God is by our side when we face the difficulties in life.

And it is worth looking to Him in these circumstances. He is there, He has things to say to us, He has the equipment ready to allow us to go along this rocky path. He loves us, He goes with us, He meets our needs.[13] He can transform what's dry into something fruitful. In this certainty, the enemy has no hold on us. Even death 'is defeated',[14] as we know our final destination: eternal life with God.

In trials we look to find the person responsible, and we often end up accusing God. And yet, we're forgetting that an enemy exists, and he continues to be active on this earth, hating all that brings life. Let us put things back in their rightful place. God is God, He loves us, and He wants the best for us. It was very clear to us in this situation we had been through with Juliette. Evil and suffering are not created by God; however, He knows we can experience them. In Luke 22.31 it says: "Simon, behold, Satan demanded to have you, that he might sift you like wheat, but I have prayed for you that your faith may not fail." The context is clear: Satan[15] wants our lives and does what he can to destroy us. We are covered by the

---

12 Matthew 28:20

13 Abraham's response to Isaac as he goes up to sacrifice him is: "God will provide". (Genesis 22:8)

14 1 Corinthians 15:55.

15 From the Hebrew *shatan* : the adversary. (Editor's note)

protection of God and not by a permanent immunity to suffering. God covers the protection of our identity, our destiny, but not our comfort. In this perspective, I felt able to express my feelings of injustice to God, without turning them against Him. I knew that only He can do anything.

Psalm 23 also really strengthened me along this journey: "Even though I walk through the valley of the shadow of death, I will fear no evil..." We would like to read, "I, God, will spare you from going through the valley of the shadow of death so you will go through no evil..." The valley of the shadow of death – there's nothing more horrible than this! However, in this situation, the most scary and destructive of situations, evil will not get a hold of me, I will stand firm and come out alive and victorious. I fear no evil, or the evil one. Satan won't have a hold on me because I am a child of God. God has traced this road for each of us, leaving us free to walk it at our own pace, but He is holding us in His hand until the end. By placing our confidence in Him, we have nothing to fear, whatever happens. What a wonderful promise!

It is worth noting that verses in the Bible can become fully real in our challenging circumstances, as though everything makes sense through these difficulties and that the power of God becomes tangible in contrast with our weaknesses and our limits.

When we heard the news of Juliette's illness and all through this process, the question of 'why' obviously came up. Why did God not prevent Juliette's condition? I don't have a complete answer to this question, and by talking with others around me, I have the impression that there are many of us questioning God about this! What I can understand at my level, is that He could have prevented this trisomy at the start of conception, because He is able to do anything. We simply wouldn't have known about it. I actually think that a lot of miracles happen, that many accidents are prevented by His hand without us even being conscious of them. In the case of Juliette, even though He didn't stop the illness, He allowed us to see Him at work and for us to testify of His presence, even though we would have, of course, much preferred a different outcome. For me, being aware of all this helps me to face the question of *why* with all its pains.

I like the metaphor: our lives are in the hands of God, like a craftsman making a tapestry. He spends His time and all His energy in the making of the work, knot after knot. These knots look like a senseless mess, until the day the craftsman flips it over. We then discover with Him this unique magnificent piece. I think that there are events in our lives which can at first seem to have no sense and yet, they contribute to the working of this piece that is made to measure and conceived by God, the craftsman of our lives.

Really, for us, the question of 'why' was not a trap. Not that it didn't come up, but we chose to welcome the question without turning our hearts away from the love we had for God. This love allowed us to question the 'why' without being destroyed, in freedom and safety, and hearing the answers without turning a deaf ear. And in this unlimited confidence, the 'why' makes way for the 'how': "How do we move forward with what we know? What do we do with it? What do we still need to grasp?"

A friend highlighted: In the garden of Eden there were two trees. One for the knowledge of good and evil (the 'why') and one for Life.[16] Which tree are we going to choose to eat fruit from? When we have 'eaten' enough Life, God sometimes gives us a piece of knowledge of

---

16 Genesis 2.9: "And out of the ground the LORD God made to spring up every tree that is pleasant to the sight and good for food. The tree of life was in the midst of the garden, and the tree of the knowledge of good and evil."

what He is doing. The other way around (eating from the tree of knowledge first), is a source of anguish and death.

Choosing to answer the 'how' also chases away any feeling of injustice and makes way for a family to embrace life to the full. Our journey was enriched by these answers to 'How to live with God'. I feel like I made a giant step forward in just a few months, in feeling profoundly loved, surrounded and secure.

The grieving process

"Not only that, but we rejoice in our sufferings, knowing that suffering produces endurance, and endurance produces character, and character produces hope, and hope does not put us to shame, because God's love has been poured into our hearts through the Holy Spirit who has been given to us."

Romans 5:3-5

A deafening silence

When I gave birth to Juliette, what was very painful for me, was the silence. Normally, giving birth brings forth life, the child cries out for the first time and then all the first medical care is given. But in this situation, nothing. Juliette was born without a sound... It was heartbreaking and terribly sad. My ears still search for this sound which I miss so desperately. What would her voice have sounded like? On earth, I will never know.

Once she was born, we wanted to see her. At first, I was very scared to look at her, or rather to be faced with death. I had never seen a dead person before her, and I was dreading this moment. I was afraid of the violence of the shock. And yet, the nurse told us Juliette was magnificent and encouraged us to take her in our arms, because at that very moment she was still warm. I treasure this precious moment in my memory like a jewel. It is at this time that we met our daughter and discovered her features, when she seemed like she was only asleep. I felt like through my daughter, death was not so terrifying. It is just a fact, a stage to go through. Juliette carried this reality on her face. In seeing her, we could see the peace and promise of an *elsewhere*.

The nurses suggested giving her a bath. At that point, it was as though she was still alive because the care and attention given by the medical staff was like that of any new-born. I was particularly surprised by the delicate way in which the nurses looked after her body, through the gentle gestures and affection they gave her. They spoke to Juliette directly, telling her how beautiful she was. It was both profoundly sad and at the same time tender and full of humanity. All this showed that we were parents to this little girl and that Juliette truly existed as a baby. Once she was washed and placed in her basket, she seemed like she was sleeping, beautifully swaddled in her covers. There was life in this little inert body. I didn't see death, but my daughter, asleep. It's this picture which will stay anchored in me, a sweet and peaceful image of a sleeping child.

And Juliette was so pretty! Her little feet and hands were well-formed. Nothing hinted at any anomaly.

In the pain of this presence-absence, God left no question unanswered. He didn't leave a deafening silence, as we might have feared. While I was sharing the suffering of not having heard my daughter's voice, a friend encouraged me to ask God what the sounds in heaven were. Maybe on earth silence reigned; but in heaven, it was a huge celebration seeing Juliette arrive. So, I asked to hear these sounds and this rejoicing. This reminded me of a part of the film *Horton*.[17] It's the story of an elephant, Horton, who holds a flower on which a speck of dust has

---

17 *Horton Hears a Who!* by Jimmy Hayward and Steve Martino, Twentieth Century Fox (2008), based on the 1954 book of the same name written by Dr Seuss

fallen. He discovers that this speck is actually a planet, with a significant community of people living on it. The whole way through the film, Horton tries to protect this flower that carries the planet and tries to get those around him to understand the reality of this planet that no one can see. The only way for people to understand that this planet exists, is to get every one of its inhabitants to make a noise at the same time, by every means possible: so that the sound produced by these tiny beings would eventually pierce through the air and reach the most sceptical of the elephant's friends. The final scene shows the people of this tiny planet who try to make the loudest noise with their voices and instruments, by shouting with one voice: "We are here! We are here." The film finishes with this moral: "A person's a person, no matter how small."

This passage is striking for the power of voices that rise up. In watching it again, I really felt the joy of heaven when Juliette arrived there. And more than anything, my ears were filled with a new sound. The reality of heaven and life after death became tangible. I can see Juliette dancing in heaven, interacting with God and laughing. And these images soothe my mothering heart.

How I experienced grief

Isn't it human and yet an illusion to believe that we can have command and control of our lives?

Before the diagnosis about Juliette, I felt like my life was riding by, like I was on wheels, not having to force anything. A child, then a second within a perfect timeframe: with a two-year gap, just like I'd planned it. I wanted to dedicate myself to motherhood, it was ideal, it flowed, I felt carried, invincible. Raphaël was growing well, I was pregnant again just like I wanted to be. The mechanics were running, everything was going as it should. Our move to Scotland couldn't have gone better, no shadow seemed to darken our path and certainly not with this pregnancy. In these moments when all is 'going well', expecting a problem is a vice to eradicate. It's like feeding negative thoughts when life is beautiful. I felt like the world was mine, everything seemed easy and accessible.

Then came the shock of Juliette's condition and her predictable death. Like a bomb explosion, it came and broke this perfect picture of my life which had been peacefully drawn before my eyes.

I had to let go of the feeling of being in control of the events and welcome my vulnerability. This is what I experienced so deeply through Juliette. Nothing was controllable anymore; everything became dramatically incontrollable, and a dark future awaited us. And yet, the life and joy we were aspiring to, flowed again. Juliette led me to welcome her for who she was, for what she carried, hoping for the best, while accepting what was. For me, that's where the miracle is.

When I think of grief, I think of a tightrope walker. Everything is down to posture and keeping your eyes straight ahead: whatever you do, don't look down, or else you fall. Moving forward along the rope, sometimes reaching resting stops, then starting to move again to then reach the end of the line. In the same way, for me, the aim was to look at the pain of the loss, without being taken over by the strength of emotions which would make me lose my footing.

Expecting a child is expecting to bring life, it's expecting an encounter with them. Giving birth to a lifeless baby is unnatural. Being faced with this lifeless body, carrying her without feeling her move, placing Juliette in a coffin, all these moments, I never wanted to go through them. When a film is hard to watch, you can just press the '*stop*' button or close your eyes and move on to something else. With this, it wasn't possible. We had to face the coldness of death, say goodbye to our daughter, leave her.

Just like the Bible says, "*there is a time for everything. A time to weep and a time to rejoice*".[18] When Jesus found out that His friend Lazarus was dead, He cried.[19] Through His tears, He proved to the world, as the Son of God Almighty, that having emotions is not a sign of weakness. If Jesus Himself cried, what greater reason for us to be allowed to do the same. Jesus connected with the emotions of grief in the present. He was fully in the present. He waited for four days[20] before going to His friend's tomb. He was grieving and not projecting Himself four days into the future where He could bring Lazarus back to life and rejoice with His loved ones. Four days where Lazarus' friends had cried and started grieving, without knowing Lazarus would come back to life. Four days when His loved ones maybe turned against Jesus, in anger, lamenting, feeling abandoned: "Lord, if you had been here, my brother would not have died."[21]

All these questions mix together actually: why didn't Jesus intervene to heal Lazarus, who was His friend? All these *whys* come and torment and overwhelm us. Why four days in which the miraculous has no place, where only the emptiness left by death remains? Why four days to experience the pain of grief, to then be met by the One who can do anything? Why four days one after another, to in the end be delivered?

The sadness of the absence of Juliette was felt over time. Insidiously, unperceived, this sadness set in inside

---

18 Ecclesiastes 3:4.

19 John 11:35.

20 John 11:34.

21 John 11:21,32.

of us. Because of all that we weren't able to do with her: hearing her voice, being able to interact with her, taking care of her. All these voids in our day-to-day took root and snuffed out the pure joy we felt during the pregnancy.

It was hard to make plans without her when I had carried her for 8 months and imagined a future with her. We had to rebuild differently, forget our plans with her and piece a new story together. Grieving Juliette was also grieving my expectations of what Baptiste and I had planned for our family. I dreamt of having children close in age, who would have had a close interaction from the beginning. With Juliette's death, I've learned to let go of these expectations. It's painful and liberating at the same time. I'm realising little-by-little that closeness isn't always to do with age. More than anything it's the family atmosphere, wanting to be together which makes us feel close and makes family a loving and comforting place where it's good to be together.

During the grieving process, I read a book which really spoke to me in that season; it describes how grief works and our capacity for resilience.[22] The authors explain that grief carries three traps to avoid:
- Believing that what is happening is our fault;
- Believing the suffering will last forever;
- Believing that what is happening to us will affect every area of our lives.[23]

I personally found myself in those first two categories at different stages of my journey: it's true that at first, I felt guilty. I had lost control and before grasping it, I felt like I could have changed something about the situation. Even though, with reason, I *knew* trisomy 13 could not be brought on by my doing, subconsciously I felt guilty, and I

---

22 S. Sandberg & A. Grant, "*Option B : overcome adversity, be resilient, regain the ability to be happy*", Michel Lafon, 2017.

23 Ibid, p.15-29.

projected this guilt onto parts of my daily life. Little things took on much bigger proportions and created feelings of insecurity and powerlessness. Quite quickly, I felt a profound tiredness come over me; I was carrying guilt like a heavy weight on my shoulders. I started questioning this feeling and gradually realised that I didn't need to feel guilty. However, realising that I couldn't change anything about what I was going through only grew the internal tiredness. It was as though, subconsciously, I was trying to repair the situation, to bring about different outcome. Then, I allowed myself permission to think that I had done my best, with all my heart, looking for the best for my daughter and my family throughout my pregnancy. I couldn't add or take anything away, nor change how things unfolded.

But this change took time. At first, I spent my time constantly losing things and looking for them. The feeling of loss had become real in lots of everyday things. Not being able to find my things left me feeling insecure and powerless. At first, I didn't really understand what was happening. A friend explained that most of the time we experience grief through present events, whether they are minute or significant. While we are experiencing the grieving processes (denial, anger, sadness, resignation, acceptance), these same emotions come and crystallise in insignificant events in the present, which in the end have nothing to do with the main issue, which of course is the loss of a loved one. Being able to decode this phenomenon allowed me to take a step back from what we were living and recognise that the emotion was linked to the grieving process.

Thanks to this enlightenment, little-by-little, I started to piece things together one with another and understand what was happening to me. My emotions of grief were expressed through everyday annoyances. Knowing this, I was able more easily to take a step back, and concentrate on what was really hurting, which was the disappearance of my daughter. Understanding this didn't take anything away from the pain but at least it didn't add on an extra layer of issues that aren't really problems, but which can grow out of control when combined with what is really troubling us.

After Juliette's death, we were well supported. The support from our loved ones and the acknowledgement of the faithfulness of God in our story kept us joyous and thankful for several months. I was also full of gratitude for Juliette's life, for all the joy she had passed onto us, all the hope and life. Then, as time went on and the reality of the drama intensified, I felt new emotions. The emptiness of death, raw in all its absurdity took hold in me, like a profound and painful tearing inside. The dead partner leaves a widow, dead parents leave an orphan. A dead child leaves…? Whatever culture you're in, there's no name for this and this anonymity expresses well the intensity of the pain.

Comparison also made me suffer. Not at the start, but this tendency made an entrance around 6 months later. For example, seeing friends or mums with their new-borns and thinking that I was deprived of this closeness. Comparison fed a sense of injustice: "Why them and not me?", "Why is it so simple for others and so complicated for me?" I found it difficult to see our friends' families grow while ours had suddenly shrunk.

It's also complicated to grieve a child I only knew in my tummy. I had imagined her but never seen her with my own eyes alive, playing, communicating. I don't even know the sound of her voice. This feeling accentuated the emptiness and powerlessness. I also needed to talk about her a lot to keep her alive and real.

The awareness of the disappearance of Juliette was constantly with me and remained there, my eyes resting only on the aspects of lack in my life or on an accentuated feeling of pain which prevented me from imagining a future where I would be free and happy. Seven months after Juliette's death, I became aware of this and took a leap. Yes, her disappearance was sad, but my life wasn't over. Every day brought good things with it, and I had hope that I'd once again bring forth life. A door was opening, and I could glimpse a bright future. Reconnecting to thankfulness helped me to lift my head and look forward. It was as though light was piercing through dark clouds. I was starting to see more clearly again, to rejoice once again.

Like little bombs

During this grieving process, I can't say I was sad all the time, it was more like little bombs exploding in my heart without warning.

For instance, after Juliette, I started painting. I had never had lessons before and so I gave myself freedom to just express inner emotions through my paintbrush. Painting in private did me a lot of good.

Several months later, innocently assuming that I had come out of this visceral grief, I signed up for a painting class. I started painting with students and a teacher, and suddenly, I felt a wave of uncontrollable anxiety come over me. I felt as though my internal wound was exposed for all to see in front of all these strangers and I was losing all my privacy. I wasn't expecting to react this way and I had to shorten my painting session to regain my composure. In hindsight, I understood that in my context, the benefits of painting were effective for me only privately and that I would quickly feel vulnerable if I did it in a group.

One day, we were in a toddler group. One of the mums had just had a baby and was introducing her child to the group. Raphaël was so excited and asked to hold the child. The mum placed her new-born in his arms and seeing him so happy, I couldn't hold back the tears. I felt simultaneously moved and overwhelmed by a feeling of injustice. Raphaël should have had these moments and this joy every day with his little sister. It hurt to witness this without being able to change the course of things. To swallow this pill of "this is how it is" without being able to change the situation.

Raphaël at only 2 years old, had this season of surprising sensitivity. For instance, I can think of a time where he must have noticed my heavy heart. He came up to me and placed a doll in my arms. Looking at me he said, "Here you are, mummy, a baby." He must have seen my pain. His thoughtfulness and tenderness overwhelmed me.

Personally, even though my whole being longed for a child, it was emotionally hard to carry a new-born in my arms. One of my friends got pregnant towards the end of my own pregnancy. I was genuinely happy for her, and I could clearly see the differences between her situation and mine. However, when she asked me if I wanted to hold her baby, so soon after the birth, emotions surfaced which I hadn't expected. Naturally, I wanted to hold him. Delighted, she placed him in my arms. I was so submerged by flashbacks of my Juliette just after she was born, so much so that I couldn't be with this new-born without also reliving the past. It was too painful and invasive. A year after Juliette's disappearance, the flashbacks were still coming, but they were different. I could have them without being invaded by sorrow. Hope had taken over from sadness.

When, at church, I heard the songs which we had chosen for Juliette's funeral, the pain would wake up inside of me, without warning. Similarly, when people prayed for difficult pregnancies, or for a pregnancy to lead to a baby without defects and born full term. Hearing these words instantly plunged me back into these months where we hoped for change for Juliette and where in the end, we had to face death. I felt sadness mixed with shame and a sense of failure remembering these same prayers uttered for Juliette which were never fulfilled. These words would come and rub salt into my wound, and I had to face the irrevocable reality again that I could do nothing more for my daughter.

I often felt exposed and vulnerable during the year of mourning. I just wanted one thing: to go and hide and retreat from social life, at least for a while. Having recognised this, I limited the time I spent in groups and focused on time in smaller settings, with close friends and loved ones who knew or were sensitive to what I was going through. I went through this whole season slowly, to take care of myself and to be aware of my limits, without adding to the pain. My sociable nature allowed me to stay connected with others, while also respecting these times of withdrawal and heart searching.

My internal judgement system was very active, bordering on over responsive. I had to reinvent myself, to create something around the emptiness inside me, but I didn't know quite how to. I felt an almost subconscious pressure that left me thinking that I wasn't making "enough" of it or not doing it "like I should". I even felt like this pressure was put on me from the outside, although it wasn't. Because of these demands, I set the bar ever higher, feeling as if I would never attain a goal that was out of reach and which, moreover, I was unable to clearly define. Once I understood that the 'project' which

I was running after had simply disappeared, I grasped that there was no point looking to create something that was never coming back. I think that was the point I truly faced the reality of grief and that I welcomed this feeling of emptiness that had settled in. Welcoming it allowed me to face it head on and to come to terms with it, at my own pace and without forcing myself.

We had been warned that birthdays or family celebrations could exacerbate our pain. Juliette died at the end of May, so the first family celebration was Christmas. It was true that, although it was festive, celebrating Christmas that year was emotionally loaded and made us feel Juliette's absence cruelly. During the meal, we went around the table so that we could each share what we were grateful for in the year 2017. I needed to talk about my daughter and honour her life, with a heart heavy with sorrow and thanksgiving. Speaking this aloud and bringing this year full circle by acknowledging my daughter's life did me a lot of good. I think that this moment sparked a change of perspective, allowing me to see the year to come in a new way.

All in all, the challenge allowed me to better behold what was inside of me and I became kinder to myself. Our friends and family were unanimous in allowing me the time I needed to grieve. For me, however, feeling acknowledged and understanding my inner workings allowed me to experience deeper healings, sources of comfort and inner transformation.

Revisiting what was dead in me

Through Juliette and through grief, I revisited moments in my life from the past and I understood that grief affected multiple layers in my life. Even though I was already experiencing a very present grief, I had to handle the emotions linked to previous experiences of grief. The darkness of Juliette's death came and shone light on parts of my life that had been set aside or hadn't been dealt with.

More generally, the shock of the diagnosis and the death of Juliette made me aware of my own finiteness. With this perspective, the sense of life and the need to leave a mark in this world became all the more pressing. I felt a sense of urgency to express what I'd learned, to leave a heritage that would endure. This book is a result of this new awareness.

Juliette's death reached what was dead in me and awoke the urgency to live and to make a difference in this world, at my level. So, through her life and death, Juliette taught me that hope is indestructible.

Living in expectation

Our experience with Juliette was a learning curve for me in many areas, one of which was patience. Being able to wait was essential throughout this experience.

When we went to the 20-week scan and the anomalies were detected, we had to wait nearly a week to find out exactly what the problem was.

During the pregnancy, I was hoping that the days of Juliette's life would turn into months, and then years. At each monthly sonogram, we hoped to hear good news. Not knowing what the final outcome would be, I learned to wait and see what would happen, all the while making the necessary preparations in case she lived.

When she died, we had to move through the phase of acceptance, waiting for the big clouds to pass and to start to rebuild after this shock. In these moments of pain, anger and sadness which are a part of grief, I looked to find my internal path, to find what was vital and to draw joy from it. Taking this stance, I could see the good things that were happening to me, and I didn't dwell on what could be missing. I made myself keep coming back again and again to these internal gymnastics of choosing where to place my gaze.

A few months after Juliette's death, Baptiste and I wanted to try for a baby again. We both thought that we would get pregnant easily, given that with Raphaël and Juliette it had only taken a few short months. But time stretched on. More than a year and a half after Juliette's birth I was still not pregnant, and I was finding the wait long. It was hard to live with and painful because I desperately wanted to have several children and invest in their education. I fully enjoyed the times I already had with my son, but the wait to build a bigger family made me feel that I also had to grieve this dream.

A battle ground set in with its doubts over our ability to have other children. In these circumstances where our situation seemed to freeze it was hard to stand firm.

In this internal battle, I was still aware that my body needed time to recover. Even though I had gone through these trials with a certain strength, this event had still been difficult. As with any physical trauma, time was needed to heal. But the process seemed to be taking too long, and I couldn't change a thing.

Gradually, a new feeling appeared. Even though I hadn't fallen pregnant yet, the hope of being so someday prevailed. I measure how happy I am with what I have already received and, in the end, welcoming a new child to our family will be a gift that will add itself to our current happiness. The next pregnancy will be a new chapter, different to that which I had with Raphaël and Juliette. This child will have their own story and their own development. I am still learning how precise the 'timing' of God is: He knows what He is doing in each of our lives!

He knows our destiny and the beginning of our days. This child will come at the right moment, in God's timing, to begin their story and be joined into ours.

Focusing on fear and bad memories or on hope and trust in God will always be a choice to make.

The glory of God and the miraculous

The miraculous

> *"And going a little farther, he fell on the ground and prayed that, if it were possible, the hour might pass from him. And he said, 'Abba, Father, all things are possible for you. Remove this cup from me. Yet not what I will, but what you will.'"*
>
> Mark 14:35-36

I went through these emotions when I heard the diagnosis of Juliette's condition. I thought that there must be a solution, a way to avoid it: news like this is so painful and unbearable. If only God could have spared us this... And then gradually, following Jesus, I chose to trust and to pray that His will be done, and not mine.

From the beginning we were waiting for a miracle, whatever that would look like, but we knew that, one way or another, God would be glorified in our lives.

(Baptiste adds: *A little after the terrible diagnosis, we were each impacted by the story of Jesus who raises Lazarus from the dead. Like He said to Lazarus' sister in tears, Jesus was saying to us: "If you believed you would see the glory of God.*"[24] *These words carried us throughout this journey. We chose to believe. Believing in God's regenerative power. Jesus resurrected several people and we have heard for 2000 years of His disciples doing the same, where there is enough faith.*[25] *If God can restore, give breath and piece a decomposing body back together, then He can definitely, we thought, change chromosomes and modify DNA in each cell!)*

And at the same time, who are we to impose the way in which God should show His glory and power? Should we expect a miracle and if so which miracle?

In our faith journey, we understood and accepted that God is sovereign, He manages the world as He sees fit and reveals Himself however He wants to. We have accepted that the product of our faith, the miracle, can be different to the one we were hoping for.

This standing in faith opened a special miracle up for us which God had prepared for our family.

There was no point fretting, running here, there and everywhere looking for physical healing for Juliette. We had to hear the call of the psalm: "Be still and know that I am God."[26] We simply had to accept it. Whether He did it or not, God remains God and we love Him for who He is. Otherwise, I would have felt like a little capricious daughter ordering her father around, telling him what he needs to do and getting cross if he didn't obey. I knew that God could heal my daughter but that, maybe, He wouldn't do it.

Several loved ones told me that, through our journey, they were able to experience their own grieving process around a miscarriage or losing a child, many years ago.

---

24 John 11:40.

25 For instance, in Acts 9.36, the resurrection of Tabitha by Peter in Joppa, or in Acts 20:7-12, that of the young man Eutychus by Paul, in Troas…

26 Psalm 46:10

This time with Juliette gave them time to become aware of the emotional weight of losing their own child and going through deep grief.

Listening to their testimony was a source of encouragement for me. It was clear that God had a plan, even though I couldn't grasp a single part of it! This process seems to me to be vital, even and especially when the life of the child *in utero* is very short.

I regularly asked God for precise things, I declared life over Juliette but without clutching onto any precise or narrow expectations. Death does not stop the plans of God for our lives, and we do not control Him. And yet, our prayers bore fruit. They produced a momentum in our relationship with God. Our intimacy with Him grew. I could see the importance of walking with an authentic heart that doesn't fear, sincerely expressing feelings, even negative ones, through prayer.

When a miracle happens, the sign of God in action is not necessarily the accomplishment of the result we were hoping for. It can happen, but my faith in God doesn't lie in it. If big things happen, I will be happy to bear witness to them. Yet, I will stay standing if I have to go through challenges again or support others in desperate situations. It isn't this that will change my relationship with God, nor my perception of who He is. I know He is there, and He works in every circumstance. To me that's what matters.

God works in our hearts, breathing in hope and confidence in Him. He loves us, He is good and is capable of the best in our lives. This 'best', we translate that to mean the healing of a sick child, that goes without saying. But this doesn't take into account that God works from a perspective of eternity that is different to ours. The promises of blessings include physical healing but aren't limited to this dimension. Our lives on earth are limited and life in its entirety includes heaven. What was

Juliette's entire destiny? When we're conscious of this earth-heaven space, our eyes look to her heavenly destiny. In this dimension, there is not even a whisper of failure, or of non-answers from God, or of non-accomplished plans.

During Juliette's funeral, we chose several songs to express our faith and proclaim it: 'Anchor',[27] 'Good Good Father',[28] 'Miracle'[29] and 'This is Amazing Grace'.[30] What is true in the light, is still true in the darkness. God is a good Father who takes care of His children. His grace is dazzling. He loves us and works in our lives; whatever storms may pass. God is the same yesterday, today and forever.[31]

God is faithful, He never leaves us without an answer, He will speak. Prayer is one of the ways of expressing a desire for a relationship with Him and He always honours this desire.

When we read the events of our story again, we know the best is what we have learned by our daughter's side, it's this transformation He engineered in us through her. God promises to walk with us. Jesus came to earth amongst other things to show us tangibly that He is God and that He is with us in every circumstance. Through His presence in painful moments, He transforms our heart and carries us further along.

Juliette Avenue

We decided to have Juliette cremated. We wanted to spread her ashes in a place we chose, which held special memories, a place we could go back to with our children.

---

27 'Anchor' *You make me brave*, Leah Valenzuela, Bethel Music (2014).

28 'Good Good Father' *Never Lose Sight*, Chris Tomlin (2016).

29 'Miracle' *Let it Echo*, Chris Quilala (2016).

30 'This is Amazing Grace' *For the Sake of the World*, Jeremy Riddle (2012).

31 Hebrews 13.8 "Jesus Christ is the same yesterday and today and forever."

A place which makes us think of life and joy, reflecting what Juliette gave us, our daughter, their sister.

Our initial idea was to plant a tree and put a plaque on it in memory of Juliette. We spoke about it to the chaplain of Robin House. She told us that we had permission to plant a tree in the garden, but not to put a plaque on it. Given the number of children who unfortunately die in the house each year, commemorative plaques would quickly distort the beauty of the garden. Whilst we understood their reasoning, we still wanted the tree to be recognisable from others. The chaplain spoke with the landscape gardener who asked, "What is this little girl called?" To her great surprise, learning that her name was Juliette, the gardener explained to the chaplain that she had just received dozens of oak trees. And not just any oak trees! Their roots were grafts from an oak dating from the Shakespearean period – the immortal author of *Romeo and Juliette!*[32] The gardener was in the middle of planting them, to create an avenue of oaks, which she was going to name *Shakespeare Avenue*. Hearing Juliette's name, she was astounded but didn't say anything at that time, she just said we could plant a tree in this avenue.

A few days later, the chaplain came back to tell us this surprising news: the gardener had chosen to change the name of the avenue. It wouldn't be called *Shakespeare Avenue* like she had planned, but *Juliette Avenue*, in reference to the Shakespeare's *Romeo and Juliette*: not only would there be a tree we could plant, Juliette would also have a whole avenue bearing her name!

This goes beyond what we could have imagined, thought of, or even desired. Who could have thought that an avenue of trees with centuries old roots would be

---

32 In the French translation of Shakespeare, 'Juliet' is written 'Juliette'. As the author is French, we have kept the same spelling.

created for their deceased daughter? For us, it attests to the lavishness and greatness of God.

At the entrance to this avenue, we symbolically planted our oak, Juliette's oak, which precedes all the others.

This avenue embodies the journey we went on with Juliette, physically, emotionally and spiritually. The Lord traced a way for our heart which is becoming a reality before our very eyes. He opened up a way which didn't exist before Juliette. He opened an access to heaven which we didn't have before. This road is a physical witness that Juliette existed, and that she led us to take hold of treasures of immeasurable worth from heaven to earth.

In this avenue, with our children, we will not stay static, motionless before a tree. We will walk. Just as Juliette got us walking, transformed us, we will get moving, in memory of her. This means a lot to us.

We feel like the journey is just beginning. All these young shoots from today will grow as time goes by. We are at the beginning of something which will spread over the years. Hope is profoundly anchored in us, telling us that things don't end with her little heart that stopped beating. Just like her life which continues in heaven, her life on earth will continue to bear fruit and we will bear witness to it, from front row seats.

God is the Creator; He traces a path where there was none, where there is no way. This corner of the garden, which was muddy and without any particular use, is being transformed into an avenue of oaks which will live hundreds of years. God's promises are being drawn before our eyes, like a call to believe in them and lean on them, despite the pain of the loss. This is the promise that all things work out for a good that is sometimes beyond us, and that God is capable of transforming a desert into fertile land.

A year later, we came back to this avenue of oaks in memory of our daughter. The trees had already grown a lot and the gardener had had the idea of planting wildflowers at the foot of the trees, to encourage pollination, new life.

This avenue of rich evocative oaks speaks to my heart and brings me a bit closer to God.

Life with an eternal perspective

Our parenting role

"For you formed my inward parts; you knitted me together in my mother's womb.

I praise you, for I am fearfully and wonderfully made.

Wonderful are your works; my soul knows it very well.

My frame was not hidden from you, when I was being made in secret, intricately woven in the depths of the earth.

Your eyes saw my unformed substance; in your book were written, every one of them, the days that were formed for me, when as yet there was none of them."

Psalm 139:13-16

God is our Father and the Creator of all humanity. For parents, it's deeply moving to realise that God makes us partners in His creation. I believe that God chooses to trust us and gives us all the tools needed to lead our children into becoming who they are. Knowing that I collaborated in the creation of Juliette thrills me and helps to chase away the sadness of the emptiness she left. She is physically absent, but fully alive in heaven. I believe that she has fullness of life, 'up there'. Taking this in changes everything.

Without fertilisation, a child wouldn't exist on earth, or in heaven. And yet God chose us to be co-creators. What an immense privilege to team up with Him from the beginning of life!

We teach our children to listen to God so that they are able to hear Him for themselves and grow in this relationship. So, I think that in looking for joy and the presence of God during the pregnancy, Juliette was also able to meet her Creator.

The final objective is that our children flourish in this relationship with God, knowing *who* they are and *what* they were created for. We also felt the heart of God thanking us for agreeing to collaborate with Him to bring forth Juliette and get her ready to live in heaven, with a view of eternity.

In our journey with Juliette, I don't have any feelings of failure or that something is unfinished. I feel I went to the end, having done my best for her by bringing her joy, love and confidence in God, all the days of her life. At the start, naturally, the best that we imagined, as parents, was for her to be healed. However today, the most important thing is to know that she's living life in all its fulness near the Father. It's an absence for us, but it's the best for her.

What an honour it was to have participated in this by choosing life and experiencing the comfort of heaven so we could face the events, filled with joy and hope for her. We experienced exceptional grace, which is beyond us, we are very aware of it.

I'm at peace knowing she went from a cocoon of love to another even bigger cocoon which will be her dwelling place for eternity. We couldn't have wished for a better life than that of living in happiness. The happiness of knowing she is unconditionally loved and welcomed.

Life, whatever its length may be, comes at a cost

Once we took on Juliette's condition and we moved forward hoping for life for her, we also took on the perspective that God had on the life of our daughter, on our lives. He opened up this dimension of eternity that concerns us all. We have measured how precious life is, whatever its length may be or whatever the anomaly.

As Psalm 139 says above, the Creator sees us when we are only an unformed mass.

This was our experience as parents. The life of our child started on the day of conception. This child to be born becomes real in our hearts the day we discover they are well and truly conceived, present in the womb. This consciousness becomes even more tangible the day of the ultrasound scan when we see and hear the little heart beating. For us, Juliette existed from the beginning. I recognised the first signs of pregnancy even though she was only conceived three weeks earlier. She had her place in our family and our hearts rejoiced from that very moment.

What happens to those children whose gestation is interrupted by a miscarriage? It's an experience which often happens in silence, as though there were nothing to be said. Personally, I'm not comfortable with the tradition in which a newly pregnant woman is told to keep the secret until the twelfth week. A pregnancy is medically declared at 14 weeks. A child born before full term is entered in the register of births from 22 weeks of pregnancy. This is the data which attests of the child's existence. Yet the heart starts beating at the sixth week of conception and the brain develops in the seventh week.

The word 'miscarriage' says a lot of the perception of a failed pregnancy. What is missed in this situation? Is it missed for everyone? I've heard it said, "Don't tell anyone about your pregnancy, it'll bring back luck." In what way does announcing life bring bad luck? Personally, I think it's wise to choose who to share this joy with, because a pregnancy can be fragile and can end. Telling everyone will needlessly expose us to insensitive words and can put the future parents in a delicate situation if they experience loss.

And yet, choosing to hide the pregnancy from 'fear of bad luck' is a type of superstition. It's as though there is a shame somewhere. It would imply that, during a miscarriage, the loss is associated with denying a life which could have been. Not talking about it allows us to live as though nothing happened. But is this really the case? And really, what message do we then pass on to the parents grieving this child they wanted? An insidious shame of having failed to bring life is the model, associated with a forbiddance to talk about it. This is doubly burdensome!

What would my daughter look like today? What sort of child would she have been? Pregnant at 4 weeks or, as the case may be, 36 weeks, the question is the same to me. The length of the pregnancy doesn't change a thing in this reality where a child could have existed, shared our life, grown our family. An embryo, then a foetus has an unmissable vocation to become a new-born.

When the verdict of Juliette's condition was announced, we felt in our relationship with God that He was giving us the choice as to whether to continue the pregnancy or to end it. Juliette was already a part of our family, it was obvious that we would keep her, whilst trembling at the idea of facing a disability so heavy that it would inevitably lead to death. But we felt that God was reassuring us and that He would not abandon us in the choice we would make.

We moved into this space of choice. Even if we had chosen to end the pregnancy, knowing we had this freedom was extraordinary. Because God loves us and wants us to be free, He allows us to investigate every option, to be fully active in the final decision. In His great gentleness, He makes us fully free to say *yes* or *no* but, in any case, He expects a sincere answer from us.

For me, it wasn't a question of me doing 'right' or 'wrong'. It wasn't a question of religiosity or moral code. In one or the other choice, the point was to collaborate with God and move forward, because, whatever the decision, it would have consequences for our lives and would position the rest of the journey.

I sincerely believe that God does not judge us in the decision we make, inasmuch as we have involved Him in the decision. If shame shows up, it doesn't come from Him. In the case of an abortion, for instance, people feel the sadness and violence of the act itself, but if their decision haunts them, trapped by an evil conscience, that does not come from Him. For us, the situation was difficult in both scenarios. But we never thought that God was imposing on us to keep life and that He would punish us if we didn't. He is not cruel!

He makes us partners in His grace whatever the decisions we take. How wonderful to think that we have a Father who gives us a choice, respects our freedom and uses us to collaborate in His work!

Of course, God cherishes life and wants to preserve it, but it isn't a menacing dogma: we especially experienced throughout this difficult choice a relationship of trust and partnership with Him.

The book of pictures and Juliette's plane

We experienced something rather extraordinary with our 90-year-old neighbour. She was aware of my pregnancy and was very happy at the idea of the arrival of a new-born in the neighbourhood. Because she was hard of hearing, I chose not to fill her in on the situation with Juliette. I couldn't see myself shouting down the stairwell what was going on with Juliette and what we were to expect. And then in the end, rejoicing with her about the possibility of the life of my daughter, even for a brief moment, did me good.

The news of Juliette's death really saddened and surprised her because she wasn't prepared for it. It happened that, on the day she heard the news from Baptiste, her 22-year-old granddaughter was at her house. When they spoke together about Juliette, the young girl remembered that in Alaska where she grew up, she had made, aged 6, a book of pictures, in the context of her French classes. These pictures told the stories of a little French girl, month after month and she seemed to remember calling this little girl *Juliette* (written the French way, and not the English way *Juliet*).

The granddaughter and my neighbour went off to look for this box, which had all her books and children's drawings in it... They were in fact at her Scottish grandmother's house. They then found this book telling the story of a little Juliette, over the years: Juliette with her pigtails, Juliette in autumn, Juliette opening her Christmas presents, Juliette skiing, Juliette at Ascension Day, Juliette at the beach...

They decided to give us the book, telling us how the connection with our story was so moving.

One of these drawings, on a loose page slipped between the pages of the book, depicts a red robin, precisely the name of the house that welcomed us after Juliette's death.

Everything in this story is improbable and yet is in fact real. These pictures come like a message that Juliette really existed and that she could have lived these moments depicted by these drawings. It's striking to realise that, 17 years earlier, God inspired this little girl in Alaska so that she would draw the story of little Juliette. We received this book as a wonderful encouragement. Juliette lived briefly, but she truly has a story, her story, and this was meticulously prepared, at least 17 years beforehand!

Some friends from France came to visit us, a few weeks after Juliette died. They felt how much of an immense soul Juliette had and that she was now really active in heaven. Life in heaven after we die is mysterious for us who haven't yet gone to 'the other side'. I think though, that we all have a destiny in heaven with God and that Juliette is in that situation.

To illustrate what our friends were feeling, they noticed that the cockpit of their plane on their return trip had the inscription 'Romeo Alpha Juliette'. A wink to our perception of Juliette! When we get to heaven, we will see who she is to God.

Life on earth is just a passage, only a speck of dust in time and space. But with Juliette, my mother-daughter relationship is eternal. Giving life is one of the things we build on earth that lasts. We will live forever in heaven and Juliette has already begun. I like to think of her being part of the welcoming committee when we arrive up there!

After nine months

Nine months after the death of Juliette, I noticed that I had found hope and joy again. Until then, saying I was a stay-at-home mum without mentioning Juliette, was like writing off a year of my life and forgetting her existence. Now, not speaking of her doesn't take anything away, in that she is present in my heart, and she has a true place in our family. Juliette is a part of my story and nothing and no one can take this experience away.

What follows from this, is that it's not useful to talk about it with everyone. I choose who to share this with because it is still a personal area. Not mentioning her doesn't mean I have forgotten her, on the contrary, she's so much a part of my existence. I particularly notice it when I'm asked how many children I have. Of course, I answer 'one', without fearing forgetting her. But I don't want to deal with the awkwardness in which people I've just met could find themselves, by saying I have 2 children but that I lost one.

I speak of Juliette at the opportune moment, when I think this exchange will be enriching and that the person I'm talking with will be open. And I especially include Juliette in the discussion if I have the space to explain our journey and her inheritance. In any case, I don't see myself in the identity of a mother who lost her child, without a calling, without hope.

I feel much more anchored in the present again and more open to others. Hearing their difficulties and supporting them opens a way to hope, to seeing God act and bearing witness to transformations in them. I have more momentum in praying for people around me and in agreeing with them for change. My relationship with God is revived and I have a new trust in Him.

I noticed a difference in my emotions between Christmas and Mother's Day. At Christmas, I was immersed in the absence and the loss of our Juliette. But by Mother's Day, I was happy to have Raphaël by my side and I was also conscious of my daughter in heaven, and I simply enjoyed being celebrated as a mum.

Big challenges now seemed less insurmountable. I feel more solid and fed in this journey I've just been on. I am more conscious of who I am and of what I want. I am less shaken by what others think. Their point of view is just as valid, as much as mine. Each person has a different perspective because of their experience, and I have mine, unique, which can be useful to others.

This trial has led me to deepen the question of knowing what really matters to me. What are my values? What do I want to communicate with my husband? My son? To those around me? For me, the important thing is to honour life just as it is given to us, in choosing to live the best, day after day. The pressure I felt at having to take stock of my life and to prove that I was worth something has gone, along with the pressure to create, invent, to give meaning to my life. I'm living in the present moment, and I love what I am living, without taking into account what others think of me. I'm moving forward at my own pace knowing who I am. I find it easier to choose what I want to invest myself in. Whether it be in my thoughts, my relationships or my projects. Conscious that life is precious, I need to refocus on what seems to best correspond to who I am and what I want. I feel a sense of urgency, an internal pulse of life pushing me to invest in durable and useful projects.

More generally, I approach life more serenely, being less emotional. What once seemed serious or without solution in the past seems surmountable now. I know that I can go through trials without being destroyed, even coming out stronger. In this perspective, obstacles are not that anymore. When an event is weighing on my mind or bothering me, I can more easily take a step back, remembering that at the end of life, I will not remember the darker moments but rather the authenticity of the moments I lived and shared.

One year later

In memory of Juliette's birthday, Baptiste, Raphaël and I went back to Robin House. With much emotion, we discovered the beauty of the avenue of oaks and the wildflowers, which were flourishing. We walked along this path, re-living the journey we've been on, and the impact Juliette has had on our lives. Personally, I was emotional without being distraught. My heart was especially thankful to have known her, to have been her mum and to have grown so much through this trial.

When we are faced with perinatal grief, we are faced with an emptiness that seems to make no sense. In this situation, it's hard to find yourself again and to get going. However, in our story, the synergy we experienced with our loved ones was overwhelming. On every level, messages went through helping us to see that Juliette well and truly existed, that she left a real mark, material and tangible. These memories are really important to us.

Letter to Juliette

Juliette, I would have loved to have heard the sound of your voice, your bursts of laughter, to have seen your first steps, your dances, to have seen Raphaël's reaction meeting you, seeing you play together... You left far too soon and yet, you changed us forever, inviting us to focus on the important things in life. We savoured each moment with you. Seeing little girls of your age, I regularly wonder what your face would be like today, your expressions, your walk...

But knowing that now you're in the arms of the Father gives my heart as a mum peace. I know that He is taking care of you. You're living now but differently, in *another place* that we cannot see, yet one that is here, right next to ours.

Pregnant with you, I could already feel your brilliance, full of life, intrepid. I can now see you full of inspiration for numerous adventures in heaven and much more! One day, we will meet again, and it will be a party, a party without limits, full of laughter and dances.

Epilogue

It's been more than four years since Juliette left us. We have advanced on the path of healing and shared the hope and joy that her life has taught us. Thanks to Robin House and the therapeutic follow-up they offer, I was able to gradually live my grieving journey and accept what had happened to us.

Meanwhile, we continued to hope for the natural arrival of another child, something that has not happened so far. The journey of acceptance has been long and painful, perhaps even more so because I had sincerely hoped this pregnancy would come easily, thinking that I had already had my share of suffering. I found the emotional ups and downs I experienced each time I realised I was not pregnant difficult. It confused me as to why this was not happening given that I had easily fallen pregnant twice before. The feeling of helplessness, of seeing time pass, the gap widening and of not being able to do anything to overcome it was distressing. But I believe that what has been most difficult in this period is not so much the expectation but the lies that have crept in. Believing that I am not worthy of having other children; that since I have not fallen pregnant, it is because I must have done something wrong, without really knowing what; that God does not want to entrust us with other children. These lies increased as our friends around us grew their families. Seeing that it was so easy for them to conceive, seemingly confirmed to me that I was the problem.

I have slowly digested the possibility that perhaps we will not have any more children in a natural way. It was complicated to integrate it, it felt painful, unfair but little-by-little, I got used to the idea and I began to perceive the contours of my role as a mother in a new way. It started with the deep joy of already being a mother of two children and daily raising my son Raphaël, whom I cherish so much. I also realised that my mothering heart could also express itself to people around me and bring comfort to those in need. Changing my professional career by becoming a counsellor with a specialism in bereavement support and trauma therapy is the culmination of this.

More than a year ago, my book was released in France, Belgium and Switzerland in the French version, despite the context of the pandemic. This was followed by radio interviews, web TV, press articles and conferences. Talking about this journey and sharing my faith with the public has been a source of great rejoicing and blessing for our family.

What I have learned in this journey of waiting is that there is a difference between 'letting go', the process that God invites us to, to give Him our situation and trust Him whatever the outcome; and 'giving up', which takes away all possible hope and interrupts any process of change. I think I have swung between these two states of heart until I fully let go, trusting God and His love for me. Giving up has led me to doubt God's action in my life, doubt His power, lower my dreams, and no longer expect much. In contrast, letting go keeps me going in the hope that something good will happen and anchors me in this global certainty that God has a project for me, that this is not the end of the story, that I can be surprised, expect the best, because God, whatever happens, continues to weave a magnificent canvas that surpasses us. By letting myself be loved by Him, I reconnect with this assurance that He has plans for peace and not misfortune for me, for my family, and that I have nothing to fear.

Another conflict played out at the level of time. The impression that time was slipping through my fingers and that my aspirations for a larger family were moving away with it. It was both distressing and confusing, like facing a form of fatality. But during the Covid lockdown, this time aside, Baptiste and I began to consider another path, to open ourselves to the prospect of adoption. This idea was present in our hearts since our wedding day, so was a possibility for us from the beginning. However, we had not considered that this would happen so quickly in our family history.

So, we started the process to adopt one or two children from the United Kingdom and are now waiting for a possible 'match' to grow our family.

With the prospect of adoption, I perceive this period from another angle. I realise that it is precisely through this anticipation that our hearts are being prepared to welcome life in another way. It also seems to me that since conception has not taken place naturally, so far, and neither of us had a previous problem with fertility, God had another plan and that He simply expected us to align our hearts with His with confidence. Our story is woven with expectations and acceptance, which has led us to seek God above all else and welcome His surprises!

Recently, I was invited to speak about my journey as a mother at a conference. This made me realise how rich and complex my approach to motherhood was, having a natural child by my side, a child in Heaven and one or two others potentially, born first in our hearts, before joining us physically. This journey has taught Baptiste and I to better understand the Father's love from different angles. Adoption opens us to this reality and awareness that God adopted us first and by living in the knowledge of this, we expect to grasp the Father's love for us even more deeply.

I hope through my writing that I have instilled hope and shown that, on reflection, disappointments can instead take us beyond to more than what we would have expected. Be encouraged and strengthened, God is good and faithful 'til the end!

With thanks to...

This book is personal and autobiographical but it would not have reached its full completion without the intervention of some people at different stages of the writing process.

Beyond the gratitude I have towards my husband Baptiste and my beloved son for their presence and their love, my thoughts turn to all those people in Glasgow who welcomed us with such warmth. The kindness and goodness that emanate from this country and its people remain anchored in me, like a balm on my heart. We did not know each other for very long and yet you faithfully stood by us.

In this precious support, I want to thank first of all Caroline, my dear friend who committed herself to my side as soon as we received the diagnosis. Our similar experiences have united us in a very special way. In a few words, sometimes even a simple look was enough to make me feel seen and understood. Thank you for being there, faithfully, for standing by me even if it probably brought back memories. Your friendship is gold.

Thank you also to Jan and Nick for your unfailing support and the choice not to look away, to face with empathy and delicacy the situation we were facing. Your parental figure in those moments when we were away from our own played a founding role in our balance.

Beth and Claire, your support as a duo was a real blessing. I remember Beth's messages reminding me to connect with my feelings, my emotions. The regular 'how are you feeling today' messages still resonate with me, as a reminder of the importance of feeling your emotions without ever denying them.

I also think of all the parents I met in the toddler groups in the neighbourhood, and in particular the complicity with Nicola, her tears full of compassion at the time of the funeral... Your love, your gentle attention has left a deep impression on me.

Then comes Begoña, my dear neighbour friend who followed our story closely throughout the pregnancy. You knew how to translate Juliette's message into drawings. These same drawings that became the cover for the book. You had the delicacy to imagine what Juliette could have looked like... Thank you for opening us up to this perception. Your talent is without equal.

After the friends, my thoughts turn to the medical profession. The team in the Foetal Unit at the Queen Elizabeth Hospital was so thoughtful. Your ability to work with Robin House from the first six months of pregnancy meant that we felt supported, understood and listened to from the very first stages by a multi-disciplinary team who knew exactly where we were going and how to support us.

As for Robin House, I am still moved when I think of the moments I lived there. You are more than just a hospice. It has a heart, a love, a warmth and even an exceptional joy that makes this place a unique resource. Our journey would have been very different without you. Thank you, Maggie, for the thoughtful and delicate attention of renaming this avenue of oaks. Thank you, Amanda, for your empathetic support, your daily presence and your ability to listen. And thank you to all the staff who were present on a daily basis, from the social workers to the cooks, to the volunteers, such as the photographer, John. Your role and presence made all the difference.

Please forgive me, as I cannot name everyone here. There are many people who have made our journey with their generosity and comfort.

And to conclude, thank you, Maddie, for your translation skills, as well as Joanna and Denise for your kind collaboration in editing the book and capturing its essence.

About the author

AUDE LOMBARD is married to Baptiste. Together, they are parents of Raphaël and in 2017 lost their second child, Juliette, at eight months of pregnancy. They have lived in Scotland for several years.

Following this experience of perinatal bereavement, Aude turned to writing and psychology, two areas that have always fascinated her. She is now trained as a counsellor, with a specialisation in bereavement support and trauma management.

If you would like to contact Aude, enquire about grief counselling, or obtain a list of helpful resources, visit: www.juliettebook.com

About Robin House

Aude and Baptiste are very thankful to Robin House staff and the C.H.A.S. (Children's Hospices Across Scotland) for their extraordinary caring support.

For over twenty years C.H.A.S. have been offering a full family support service for babies, children and young people with life-shortening conditions. This includes palliative care, family respite and support – through their hospices, homecare services and hospital presence.

The C.H.A.S. is reliant on gifts, donations in kind, and donations in time. Please consider joining us in supporting their amazing work. Visit them at: www.chas.org.uk

Children's Hospices Across Scotland

Printed in Great Britain
by Amazon

35682083R20066